BE A BOSS WHO
GROWS LEADERS

— EXPERIENCE THE PLEASURE & REWARD OF —
HELPING PEOPLE GROW INTO CAPABLE MANAGERS

PAT WIESNER

First Edition
10 9 8 7 6 5 4 3 2 1

Cover graphics and design by Laura Pilz

Published by BookBaby
7905 N. Crescent Blvd., Pennsauken, NJ 08110

ISBN: 978-1-09836-739-8

Foreword

By Eliza Cross

When I was a new sales director in my early 20s, I was as green as I could be about how to manage a successful team.

For example, I thought the way to be a good salesperson was to talk confidently about my product. I thought the primary role of a strong manager was to give orders. I thought the best leaders knew how to get people to follow them and execute their vision.

And then I met Pat Wiesner.

From the first day I started working with him, Pat upended my notions about selling, leading, and running a successful company. He taught me things like:

- Listen more than you talk.
- Be a problem solver.
- Share the credit.
- Help people see their strengths.
- Keep your promises.

For 30 years, Pat wrote a monthly column for *ColoradoBiz* magazine and transparently shared his thoughts and real-time lessons about running a business. Month after month, through good times and bad, he wrote about topics like hiring and motivating good people, managing cash flow, being an exceptional salesperson, dealing with competition, building a team, and leading a successful company.

Pat has the gift of writing like he talks, and his words resonated with readers. People tore his articles out of the magazines and forwarded them to others. His columns were posted on company bulletin boards. Employees snuck them on their managers' desks.

Pat's articles were always the highest-scoring pages in *ColoradoBiz's* reader surveys. Whenever I was at a business event, it seemed like someone would say, "You work for Pat Wiesner? I love his columns. He must be a great guy to work for."

Hindsight is a wonderful thing, isn't it? I don't think I fully appreciated my luck in working for a truly extraordinary boss until I left after 16 years to start my own company. I soon discovered that not everyone was as unfailingly honest, encouraging, open-minded or transparent as my friend Pat Wiesner.

A couple of years ago I was asked to share a few words for a tribute video to Pat that WiesnerMedia produced. Suddenly emotional, I fought back tears to say what was in my heart: "You changed my life."

It was true. Pat's encouragement and the lessons I learned while working with him helped me be a better listener, a better business owner and a better communicator.

It turns out I'm not the only person he touched. Pat modestly shared some of the many notes and letters he's received over the years from other employees he similarly influenced:

"I wouldn't be where I am today without your encouragement and belief in me."

"Thank you for giving me the opportunity to have such a wonderful life working in this industry."

"This is my 37th year working with the magazine. I'm so grateful for everything. Thank you!"

"You affected our family more than you can possibly imagine."

The essays in this book represent the best of the best of Pat's many articles, drawn from three decades of building a successful, resilient company that continues to thrive today by helping its people grow.

Economies fluctuate, people move, and technology advances, but the essence of great leadership really doesn't change very much. Whether you're as green as I was when I started in business or a seasoned corporate veteran, you'll be challenged and inspired by Pat Wiesner's thought-provoking words and ideas.

Author's Note

Most of this book was originally written as short articles for monthly editions of *Colorado Business* magazine and its successor, *ColoradoBiz*, from 1989 until recently. These columns were very successful during those years, and we kept getting the suggestion that they would really be worthwhile if we presented them in a book format.

When I looked at the collection of articles, I had to agree. These are real examples drawn from real learning situations in management growth. They make more sense in a book, where they reinforce and underscore each other. Readers see them all coming together in a mutual dependency that quickly and easily educates them about real deep understanding of management principles.

It became clear that these short but true examples were cut from the fabric of real business life. The message is always obvious and the action required makes sense. This is not dependent on doctorate-level business school advice but is about common sense and knowledge about how people process information and react.

How often have you heard things like, "Those engineers (or sales people or ...) are hard to motivate!" This book has some good ideas for you.

If you like people to the extent that you are genuinely interested in their success and you don't think that you have to know everything and give every order, you can be the best boss that the people working for you ever had! You will also become a better boss than you ever expected you would be.

It all comes down to understanding the simple rules of becoming the best boss you can be. The ideas are easy to "get" and fun to apply.

None of us is very far from being good at successfully managing others. Read on and see!

Table of Contents

The Best Advice I Ever Got

A simple formula for building relationships with people

It wasn't a tip to help me make a million in the stock market or the secret to a big sale that made the company. The best business advice I ever got was a simple idea on how to treat people. It has always stuck with me.

Back in the early '60s when I first got into the publishing business, I was basically an engineer by training, trying to learn how to sell advertising space in a technical magazine. To help put me on the right track, my sales manager sent me to the Dale Carnegie Sales Course. The classroom was in a building on Michigan Avenue in downtown Chicago.

I loved it!

It was all brand new to me.

What made people buy? How do you make your product stand out in your prospect's mind? What is closing, and how do you make sure you are doing it right all the time? Slowly it began to sink in that good selling wasn't so much telling people about your product as it was finding out about their problems and then trying to help them find solutions.

Eventually I took every kind of sales course available. It became sort of a way of life for me because it was helping me become successful. Along the way I ran into an instructor by the name of Bob James. He had a great influence on my life, although I haven't seen him in 40 years. I'm sure he had a great influence on a great number of lives. Bob's personal formula for building people relationships was this:

Help people see themselves in light of a strength of which they are unsure or unaware, hopefully related to the person they dream of becoming.

Since I was trying to make it in business and management, it is there that I applied these ideas. It turned out to be the best advice I ever got and, in my opinion, the best advice I can give to someone trying to make it as a manager.

The reason it is so powerful is that the manager must find out who the managed "dreams of becoming," and then he or she must look for and find strengths the managed person is "unsure or unaware" of. This is hard work! But nothing short of this hard work will enable you to get the best out of people.

If you are my boss (and a great manager) and you find out that one day I'd like to start my own company (or be a sales manager or teach a class or run for office) you will start looking for strengths in me that will enable me to reach my goals and then you will tell me about those strengths!

When I discover that you are truly trying to help me achieve my goals, I will in turn give you the best work I am capable of. I will want to earn more of your support.

It is a bit arrogant to say that a great manager is one who builds people. It is more acceptable to me to say that a strong manager is one who works hard to find out the goals and ambitions of the people working for him or her, who then looks for strengths and abilities in this person, and who then talks to the person about these abilities and reinforces them.

As we believe more in the strengths and abilities of which we are unsure, we grow.

o o o

Relax!

Whoever said, "Don't sweat the small stuff' was right.
And it's all small stuff.

While driving to work this morning, I ended up in a long, stop-and-go line waiting to get through a red light.

A combination of our ever increasing early-morning traffic and construction limited a usually easy corner to one lane. The line stretched for a half-mile or more.

I did what everyone was doing. I got into line and stewed as if this whole thing was a distraction specifically designed to frustrate me. I began to take it personally.

With nothing else to do, I occasionally glanced at my side mirror to see how long the line was becoming. Eventually, I moved forward enough to where I was sure I would get through on the next green light.

One more glance in the mirror revealed an SUV (one of those with sinister dark windows that make you think it's driven by Darth Vader or Charles Manson). He had left the end of the line and driven past everyone waiting their turn. He stopped next to me, with his blinker on. He clearly was expecting to get in front of me to go through the light.

No way! I was fuming! The light turned, and I moved quickly to ensure he couldn't take what was rightfully mine. The line stopped momentarily and the SUV driver extended his hands, palms up in a gesture of supplication.

I hollered something through my window about him returning to the end of the line where he belonged, now and for the rest of his life. He flipped me off, I thumbed him to the rear, and with a sneer in full bloom and pulse hammering, I forced him back behind me and beat him through the intersection.

Victory! He turned at the intersection and was gone.

As I drove on and cooled off, I began to wonder what the heck happened. It was so stupid that it was embarrassing. Here I was, a 62-year-old, otherwise mild-mannered business publisher, ready to shout obscenities and do battle over a place in a line of cars with someone I didn't even know.

For all I know, the guy may have had an emergency.

By the time I got into the office, I still was thinking how I wished I had acted differently. Then a problem arose that made me forget the drive to work. It was one of those frustrating situations where there is no good solution. A customer was denying we had an agreement and was refusing to pay for his advertisement.

I was just starting to get hot when I was told of an ex-employee who was suing us. I just got hotter.

Wait! I don't want to live like this!

I immediately sat down and wrote a list of things I would do differently from now on:

- I will accept as my No.1 job in life, a job I enjoy greatly, to deal positively and easily with situations that give others high blood pressure.
- Instead of being controlled by circumstances, I will be in control.
- A calm, pleasant, understanding manager is first a calm, pleasant, understanding person.
- This will not be easy and must be worked on every day.

I hope I run into the same guy tomorrow in line at the light, so I can see what it will feel like to let him and his anxiety crash the line, and get my day off to a better start.

o o o

The Same the World Over

When done right, basic salesmanship is a pleasure.

We were tired, my wife and I, after a long day of touring on foot the ancient and interesting city of Antigua, Guatemala.

It was late afternoon; it was pleasant but still fairly warm, and we had just sat down on a bench overlooking all the bustling activity in the "Parque Central." Out of the corner of my eye, however, I could see them coming for us, and I thought to myself, "There goes our moment of relaxation."

After a few days' stay in a third-world country like Guatemala you get used to the constant entreaties of the indigenous people, in this case the Mayans.

They are a wonderful, talented and happy people, and, in all the time we were in their country, even though they occupy the lowest rung on the economic and social ladder of Guatemala, not one of the natives ever asked me for a handout. But they sure did try to sell us lots of stuff.

The Mayans weave textiles just as they have done for centuries. They use a "back strap" loom with one end tied to a tree or some other such anchor and the other end wrapped around the weaver's back so that the actual weaving is in front of them. The results are magnificent, colorful works of art. It takes about three weeks' work on one of these looms to make a piece of cloth that sells for about $15.

And they sell mountains of this artwork to tourists.

A young Mayan girl in Guatemala might go to school for just five years before she goes to work in the family business. At age five, children begin to learn to carry baskets and other objects on their heads, and even as adults they carry their store of goods for sale on their heads and in their arms. They also learn early the language of the market.

Most can say "Good price for you! Your husband pays!" in 10 languages. Most can carry on a conversation in four or five languages, all of it learned in the marketplace.

They are a people who are extremely hard working and persistent. And they can make you dog tired.

Which brings us back to the bench in the Parque Central. I am always quickly pegged as American, and the young Mayan woman said something to me in English. I said, "No, gracias," as I had done already at least a hundred times that day.

Then, I waited for her to get into a higher gear, which is usually what happens when you are trapped on a bench. But instead, the young woman just smiled and asked me if I was enjoying Guatemala. I said yes, and she asked what I liked best.

You guessed it. Before long I was telling her about Denver and my kids and grandkids. She proudly called to a couple of little kids who had been playing in the park fountain, hers, and she told me their names. It was a fun and interesting exchange, and, of course, I happily bought a bunch of stuff from her.

She, in fact, offered me an example of the best kind of salesmanship. Instead of just pounding on me to buy, she got me talking about something I was interested in, then let the human equation take over.

If we just continually ask for the order, our customers will keep saying, "No, gracias." If we get involved with our customers, they will buy easily.

Every time I saw her in the park after that, we waved like old friends. As with all good sales, everyone had benefited.

The Secret of Leadership

Let the other guy catch a fish once in a while. And stay out of his way while he's doing it.

Fourteen down and 14 to go. Days, that is.

For two weeks, three of us have been on a boat on the Intercoastal Waterway going from Florida to Cape Cod. (How I spent my summer vacation!) It's really interesting to see what becomes important to you as your daily living space shrinks from the size of a normal house down to a trawler with a couple of cabins and a main salon.

There are the three of us on the boat, sometimes four, as my kids cycle on and off, so privacy is sometimes an issue. Most meals are prepared and eaten on board, but occasionally we have dinner ashore in marinas or nearby towns. Magnificent scenery is served up in an unusual way, sort of like the world's longest Disney-like ride with the attractions changing constantly. Miles of almost nothing except bushes and trees and mosquitoes, deerflies (bigger and tougher than horseflies), then suddenly a small community of beautiful homes along the shores or a huge, industrialized city like Charleston (just spectacular from the water).

Everything and everybody fishes here! The people fish, of course, with thousands of different kinds of rods, reels and bait. The birds fish. Even the fish fish! I saw a bunch of fish jumping out of the water. They were about four or five inches long and schooling within a 20-foot circle. I asked someone why they were jumping, and was told they were jumping out of the water to get away from a predator. Of course, the escape was short-lived.

I also watched for a while as a man showed a young boy some things about fishing off a pier. He basically talked him through baiting the hook and then let the boy throw the line in the water and land a fish. The first bite got away, but the man kept encouraging his pupil, and the boy fished! He landed the second bite, but the fish got away as the boy tried to get it off the hook. The next one the kid landed, he unhooked safely, put it in his creel and then excitedly told everyone in shouting distance about his catch. He also kept opening the creel just to check that his fish was still there.

What's the difference between this scene and one where a teacher baits every hook, does a proper cast, snags the fish, brings it to the boat, etc.?

Leadership!

If we would be leaders, which is more than and different from being a manager, we would grow the people around us. If we are helping the people on our team individually to feel confident and sure of themselves, to actually catch fish with their own skills, we are leaders. And what's more, we are training leaders.

The Chinese have a way of fishing with a long-necked bird, some sort of crane that normally just fishes for itself. They put a collar on it so that it can't swallow, and then put it into the water to fish. When it catches a fish, they bring it back to the boat, where, because it can't swallow, the fish goes to the owner of the bird and then the process is repeated. The interesting thing is that unless they let the bird swallow a fish himself now and then, it quits fishing.

We will be better off if we concentrate on building people rather than on making people work harder. And besides, you can't get good at something unless you have the freedom to do it yourself; make mistakes and learn.

Remember this: The people hardest to find in today's business world, and thus the most valuable, are those who have the ability to grow others rather than only shine themselves.

The Sin of Micromanagement

To discover a manager's true colors, make him a Little League coach. Then watch carefully.

E ver hear stuff like this around your place? "Around here, the only one who makes a decision is the boss."

Or, "When she assigns a project, she also tells me every step to take to get it done. I don't get a chance to think or use any of my own ideas or methods. I'm just supposed to do it the way I was told. And if I don't, I get hollered at."

The most unhappy people have to be the micromanagers of the world. I suspect they always are miserable because nothing ever gets done exactly right (their way) and they never seem to have any time. The people who work for them probably are the most bored and unfulfilled of all employees.

But you can easily study the sins of micromanagement in an interesting laboratory: sports. The "projects" are short, a couple of hours at the most. The pressure is high because success and failure are so clearly defined. In this environment, people skills or lack thereof quickly become evident.

This is soccer tournament time in Colorado. I've had occasion to watch a lot of games. It is particularly interesting to wander around a tournament and watch different coaches and how they handle teenage kids. In order to see the effects of micromanagement telescoped into a measurable short period of time, first look for a coach who is a screamer— one who is constantly shouting instructions to his team as they are trying to be loose, creative and athletic. Listen a while. "Change fields! No! No! Left foot! Look out, Billy! Pass it to Billy! No! No! C'mon, you can do better than that! No! No! Let it roll and run with it! Matt, push it through, don't keep it so long! Good stuff, Mike! Next time, go for the corner! Not so far! Pass! Pass! Now! Now!" Ad nauseam. And a lot of this often is delivered in the heat of battle in the tone and the pitch of an angry, sometimes enraged, coach.

A particular coach I observed truly wanted to choreograph every step of every player with his shouted commands. If he could have, I think he would have preferred to limit each player to the moves he wanted and nothing else. And his players knew it.

This same man went to incredible lengths to explain loudly on the sideline to one 15-year-old midfielder and anyone within hearing distance that he hadn't done as he was told, that he was not a good player and that he did not deserve to play again. All this delivered as some kind of condemnation with the force only a truly angry man can muster.

These kinds of managers, whether in business or coaching, seem to get self-esteem for themselves by taking it from others. Disgusting.

This day, this particular team lost the game 1-0. We can only speculate on what might have happened if the coach had taken the higher road and encouraged his team to be the best they could be, instead of trying to inject himself into the brain of each player like some hideous alien force.

It might take years in a business setting for a micromanager to have the same effect on a business team as this coach on his soccer team, but such a management style certainly would inhibit the team effort all along. Good people will leave, and you'll never know why; morale and accomplishment will never be what you want. It will be a problem department until the offensive manager either is fixed or removed—and fixing is nearly impossible.

Screamers rarely make good managers. If you have one or know one, get him or her help, or get them out. The kind of people whom you need to help you reach your goals usually won't develop in this environment. Managers who need to make every decision clearly are more interested in themselves than in any person they manage. The managed never will be truly motivated, and the real joy and sense of potential from being on the "team" never will be realized by anyone. Micromanagers not only are self-limiting; they also severely inhibit those around them—maybe even one of your business' potential next stars.

If we have a question about a manager or a prospective employee, maybe we should find out if he or she coaches a Little League team, then go see how the kids are treated. Whatever the treatment is, it will carry over into business.

o o o

The Seagull Management Technique

Popular for many years, this management method was once used by Attila the Hun to run an entire empire. Strangely, I was recently bitten by a seagull right here in Denver. That's what makes me write all this stuff down.

You know how it works: Some vice president comes to town and calls a meeting. Attendance at the meeting is required of everyone in the group. This "manager" proceeds to rip everyone, the project and its leaders. There aren't many questions asked, mostly a lot of "messages" delivered. Then they pack up and leave you to sort it all out.

There are only three tenets to the Seagull method of management: Swoop in. Crap on everything. Swoop out.

That is what makes it so easy to adapt to any situation. Anyone with a little power can use it.

Once I was hired as the director of marketing for a company where somehow, I got the idea that I was supposed to fix some problems overnight. Of course, I didn't understand the problems well enough to fix anything. Instead of asking questions, listening to answers and engineering solutions along with the people involved—people who knew the problems better than I—I did the opposite. You guessed it. I brought in my best "Seagull." I changed policies, redirected efforts and even fired some people. All on far too little knowledge, most of it from those who had axes to grind that I didn't take the trouble to discover.

I swooped in, and eventually I was myself swooped out. But I did learn something about management and leadership.

Although it makes for an easy joke or two, we are constantly in contact with more subtle types of Seagullism. For example, beware of management that does not ask questions. If they don't ask questions, they don't care what you think. Who wants to work where the company doesn't care what you think? Of course, the corollary to this is represented by management that always seems to have all the answers, whereas your thoughts, even if they are solicited, are never as good as theirs.

From the management side, be interested in your people and their ideas. We can make plenty of changes and make them work if we work out solutions with those affected.

If an organization changes without including the thoughts of those whose jobs are being affected, look for a Seagullist. The first effect of this is to make people feel insignificant. The objective of good management is to accomplish just the opposite. In order to get the very best work out of people, real leaders figure out how to make people feel truly significant to the work at hand.

The worst place to find Seagull tendencies is in yourself! If we don't genuinely care about the ideas, goals and aspirations of those who work for us, we undermine their confidence, decimate the work ethic, dampen the spirit, blunt their ingenuity and compromise their interest in accomplishing our objectives. Not a very good way to look out for our own interests. The worst result that accrues to the Seagull managers is that they are denied the ultimate "manager's high" of leading real people as they give their very best work to a project.

Self-image and self-confidence are very fragile in most people. A dose of Seagull will last for a long time. It gets the locals fighting among themselves, it makes people feel unimportant, and it destroys confidence.

If you see signs of Seagull behavior in your boss, realize that this person will never be a good person to work for. If you can, find another. If you suspect yourself of Seagullism, see a management doctor to get rid of it!

○ ○ ○

Silent Career Killers

Some people are good enough to achieve in spite of these things, but most of us can't survive handicaps like this.

Everybody doesn't get to be president of the company. That's obvious. But many times, the reason we don't achieve our goals is not so clear. Often, all the education, the MBAs, the midnight oil, the good luck, the genius and even sucking up fail.

Watch for some of these career killers in our own personality. I've seen quite a few otherwise good people top out way too early as a result of these, and I have been badly wounded myself a couple of times. This is not meant to be an exhaustive list, just some of my favorites. If you have some not on the list, let me know.

People who can't admit they made a mistake. I have been fired twice in my career. The first time, I was working as the marketing director for a fairly large West Coast company. I had been hired over some men who had been working for the company for a long time. After about a month, in a show of power and ego, I demoted a 15-year sales manager just to show everyone how things were going to be done differently. It turned out to be a mistake. This man was good and could have been my best ally if I'd done it right. Everyone knew, including me in my soul. But for the next year I kept insisting that my way was the right way while my credibility and effectiveness unraveled to the point where the boss and I both knew that my career there was over. The only smart thing I did was at the end of this unfortunate episode when I told the ex–sales manager that I was sorry for having screwed up his life and this company. Too late; it was after my exit interview.

If I told about the other time I was fired, it would have a similar ring to it. People whose self-image won't ever let them say, "Folks, I was wrong. Help me do this right" become isolated from real input and honest feedback. And you can't be successful with that kind of handicap.

People who can't get to work on time. Some years ago, I started a new job and asked a new friend what time work started. "Just beat the boss in," he said with a wink, "and he doesn't get here until about 10!" That is just what I did for a while until I realized that the few people who worked for me were treating me the same way and I was getting the same reputation that the boss had.

In my business life I've watched at least six "10 o'clock scholars" die on the corporate vine because of this. The fact is, it doesn't matter if you stay until midnight and if you work every Saturday and Sunday; it doesn't matter if you're smarter and work harder than everyone else in the shop. If you can't get to work on time, you lose a little respect every day you're late, and resentment builds. It builds at such a slow rate, no one thinks it's worth making an issue over. But it builds, and it will get you. You won't know why you missed out on that last promotion—or, if you're the boss, why that really good person quit and went somewhere else.

People who manage from somewhere above. I have known three managers who actually put their desks on platforms, but most have the platforms only in their minds. They write long memos dealing about everyone else's mistakes, they don't give much credit and they manage to take for themselves that which does come along. They use phrases that depreciate others like, "My people..." and "What I want you to do...." When with other managers, they are always putting down their employees. With employees, they are always giving orders. Somehow, if you work for this person, you know that he or she isn't really interested in your welfare or your future. You don't trust him or her with your aspirations and dreams.

He/she will not usually make it. And never really understand why.

The only nice thing about these afflictions is that they are totally reversible. All you need is an open mind and a willingness to change.

o o o

Are You Promotable?

Twenty top managers provide food for thought when asked what characteristics they seek in highly promotable people.

The question was, "What five personal characteristics do you look for in promoting someone?" Most agreed on some characteristics you would expect.

For example, the most promotable people would be enthusiastic, hardworking, intelligent and have a positive attitude in all circumstances. Hardly a surprise.

What is more interesting are the thoughts and suggestions that came after the obvious. Each boss expressed his or her thoughts differently, but most had the same basic ideas for us to consider. The most suggested characteristics:

The desire to want to help others become successful—the real secret of team-building. The only foolproof way to get the best work from a team is when each member knows that each other member (and particularly the chief) is interested in the personal success of all. The ability to stimulate development and professional growth belongs to the very few, the best managers, the ones who genuinely care about that development and growth and make it happen.

Some people have a way of working down to those around them. They seem to have a knack for the putdown, the "better" idea, the last word and self-promotion. This is probably the best way to foreclose on real promotion.

The person most likely to get promoted will be one who listens a lot and doesn't have to be the only one with good ideas.

All of this flows from self-confidence. It is a sign that someone has confidence when they can take the time to listen and care.

Shares the vision for success of the company. So many people work for wages and wonder why they never attain success. Although someone can be a contributor through hard work, true achievement is impossible unless one internalizes the goals of the company.

If the profit goals of a company are not the profit goals for you, the manager, you will be a mediocre manager. If you are not proud of whatever it is your company does well, if you aren't spending all your energy trying to enhance and improve this product or dimension, you will be an also-ran as a manager.

The right person for a promotion, for example, will understand the business and be instinctive about conserving resources, limiting expenses and maximizing sales.

The right person for a promotion takes ownership in the company. He or she will say "we" when things are going well and even when they aren't.

Have a sense of humor. The best bosses I ever had had a sense of humor. They were able to let built-up tension out of a situation. They could put things in proper perspective and get everyone back to giving their best effort to the solution of problems. If you're not having some fun, you're not providing the relaxed atmosphere that will get the best work out of your people.

Have a sense of what is really important in life. Business is tough. Selling is hard. Production is impossible. At times, everyone's temper will be pushed to the max, nothing will work out right, the cost will be too much, and the boss will say "get it done!" when it's impossible.

It is a valuable person who steps back and says, "Folks, it's only a job. It's just a way to make a living." It's a matter of managing the environment so people feel the pull of reality mixed with the difficulty.

So said our little panel. You?

o o o

Socrates—a Great Salesman!

He did a great job of selling ideas, but he would have been a very good chariot salesman too.

At the risk of being repetitious, I want to recall a couple of sales experiences I have already written about:

One time I was on a call with an advertising-space saleswoman, helping her set up for a presentation at a large, big city ad agency. This was to be a very big sale if we got it.

We were setting up in the 21st-floor conference room at the agency as some of the lower-level account execs began to arrive. I was very nervous, and I really didn't have much to do. Everything important about the presentation was being handled by the sales-rep on the account, but I was intensely aware of just how much business this particular agency could send our way ... or keep us from getting.

Wondering if she was equally nervous, I asked her what the strategy was.

"I'm going to find out if they like us," she told me. Before I could say any more, the top guns at this agency came rolling in and sat down.

Our presenter began: "We have set up to give you a half-hour presentation on why our magazine should be on the 'must advertise' list for five of the major accounts at this agency. If you already agree, we can skip the presentation and move on to ideas we have to help you create dynamite programs. Have you already made that decision?"

She stopped and waited.

After a few smiles passed around the table, the boss said, "You know, we have made that decision. Let's move on to other things you can do for us."

I decided then that this salesperson was going to be very successful indeed.

My wife and I recently left Guatemala after being there for four weeks. A couple of times a day during that time I crossed the town square where many Mayan Indians were selling crafts, particularly cloth, made in their villages.

I talked to one lady a number of times each week.

She sold me more than I wanted to buy, and I admired her sales ability, but the clincher came the day we were leaving.

She said, "I've enjoyed our conversations, keep healthy and be happy. Would you give me your knapsack before you leave?"

You can guess what I did.

Socrates would have loved both these people.

Why? Because they got results by asking the question that was on their mind. Socrates taught that the best way to teach was to draw lessons out of students by asking questions. Scholars now call it the Socratic Method.

To this day no one has improved on the technique for opening up people to find out what they think—leading them into a discussion around the points you want to make.

The best salespeople (and the best managers, for that matter) are the ones who not only ask questions but also know where they are going with their questions.

Questions like: What do you think? Are we going to get your business? What is your idea? What would you like to accomplish? What would it take? Why?

Ask the questions that draw the other person into the discussion you want to have.

But this also takes some preparation.

First, you have to know what discussion you want to have. Maybe you want to know if your customer has already made up his mind, perhaps you want his backpack or maybe you want to know why he likes your competition better.

If you want to ask the intelligent questions that will force your customer into becoming involved in answering them, you also have to know that customer. More work. And do that work before any other questions get asked.

Then figure out how you are going to ask your question. Ask questions, lots of questions, but particularly be sure that you ask the one you most want answered!

No matter what, get that question asked!

o o o

Happy Cooks

Unhappy cooks make lousy food. What about unhappy workers?

Sometimes a department or division's boss is the last to know when something is wrong with his or her area that could do serious damage to the department and perhaps even redirect a career.

Chef Tracy Des Jardin was on TV the other morning as I was getting ready for work. She was being interviewed by one of those early-morning smiling network faces on Good Morning USA Today America. Apparently, she owns the Rubicon restaurant in Los Angeles. Even at that hour, her food looked fantastic, inspired, her restaurant obviously "foraging central" for the elite eaters in that part of the world. One of the principal reasons for her success, she said, was that she had happy cooks. And happy cooks make good food.

Happy workers get good results.

What makes people happy at their jobs? Think about yourself. For myself, I want to know what is expected, how I will be rewarded, how I fit in, what my future is if I perform and most of all, that you, my boss, have my interest at heart.

As managers, we must know all our employees' answers to these questions to do what is expected of us: to get good results.

Why be the last one to know your department is running on the ragged edge of self-destruction? Here are five questions you can ask to help ascertain whether your employees or managers are happy in their jobs:

1. What are the top three items in your job description? Just be quiet and wait for the answer. Don't be surprised if you are surprised. You can consider yourself a very good manager if you agree on two out of three the first time you ask. Next time you ask, if you agree on the three items, ask for a couple more. However, there is little to be gained by going further.

It will comfort you to know you are managing someone who understands what is expected. More importantly, the employee will know you care and are listening.

2. Describe our team; how does it function? Nothing could be more important to you. But it doesn't matter how you think it functions. It really works the way your people think it works. So, listen carefully. If you hear words like "we" and "us" along with a sense of excitement and pride in the group, that's great. But listen for indications that what you thought was a team really isn't. Press the issue: Is this person getting what they need from you? From others?

3. Who else in this company depends on your input to do their job right? Dotted lines are harder to manage than the solid black lines on an organizational chart. You are trying to diagnose malfunctions in relationships in your organization. Listen carefully and you will get ideas on how to provide better input to this person. With this understanding, you should be able to help your employees feel in more control of what they should be producing.

4. Do you think you have a future in this company? If so, what is it? If not, why not? I will work hard in a company where I think I have a future. It's your job as my boss to help me see that future. This may be tricky; if you're tempted to be anything but honest with me, I'll see right through you. If I sense you are trying to manipulate me, I may continue to work hard because I want a job, but you will not inspire me to do my best.

If I don't have a future, let's get it on the table. We have to deal with it sooner or later, so why not now?

5. How do you feel about my commitment to you? In our company, we ask this question to start the conversation where the manager explains to the employee the extent of his/her interest in the employee's future. Again, any attempt at manipulation usually will fail. And besides, the best adhesive for a team is honesty and mutual support.

An outstanding manager asks lots of basic questions and then waits for answers.

○ ○ ○

How Can We Develop People Skills?

They are as important as any business skill, but how do we improve them? Where do we sign up for courses?

This was overheard at a business luncheon meeting as a few middle-management people discussed the success of one of Denver's well-known leaders:

"He's one of the best when it comes to financial stuff, but when you combine that with his people skills, it's no wonder that he's so good. People love to work for him."

The best sales manager I ever worked for was terrific at details. He seemed to know my accounts better than I did, conducted great meetings full of good ideas on how to sell better to tough customers, and did a great job of getting us new sales tools just when we needed them.

But he also had a knack for getting the best and hardest effort out of his people. He had wonderful people skills.

A college student recently asked, "What should I take in college that will make me successful in my career? I mean, I want to be an engineer, but you and I both know there are engineers and really successful engineers. How can I best prepare myself to be one of the really successful people in the next generation?"

The answer has to be: Develop your people skills. But the bad news is, though there are lengthy courses of study in business and engineering, there is little available (perhaps a psychology course) for teaching people skills—which will probably be more important to one's future.

And what about those of us who have been out in the real world for a while and still aren't sure how to improve our people skills?

Here are some thoughts from a good team I'm familiar with:

Take a course in human relations. There are many, but be sure to pick one that stresses genuine concern for, and commitment to, others rather than technique, which is designed to manipulate.

Conduct your own real-life class outside business. Decide that everyone you meet will be happy you crossed their path. Try to make all you meet feel better about themselves. That means every co-worker, waitress, bartender and cab driver—and particularly wives, husbands and kids. This is tougher than it sounds. We must sincerely find something we like about each of these people and tell them about it in a way they accept and believe. There is a lot more to it than "You look marvelous!"

Coach a team of kids. And decide you don't care nearly as much about winning and losing as about making all your team's kids feel better about themselves after a season than they did before it.

Talk to your peers. This list was generated by a group sharing ways to increase sensitivity to the psychological needs of others. It is not a complete list. Why not do the same in your group? If it is done with simple honesty and sincerity, much good, basic communicating is likely to happen. You'll learn something about yourself if you listen carefully.

Talk to your management. A good manager will give you honest, sensitive input about where you are in his/her estimation. And how you can improve. A bad manager will use the occasion to beat you up. Consider the source.

In any case, become really interested in others and what makes them tick. You'll find it's a full-time job that can't be turned off and on. You're either interested in others beyond what they can do for you or you aren't.

If you are, your people skills should be fine.

The Power of Lists

A ready-made, natural formula for getting our best thinking on paper. The resulting blueprint is easy to understand, communicate and follow.

Hillsdale College president George Roche asks, "Why do we make lists?" in the March 1996 issue of Imprimis. His answer: "We make lists so we will not forget what is important. But all too often we regard list-making as a trivial task when it should be our first and most important priority. For if we chronically forget items like milk and bread unless we make a grocery list, or nuts and bolts unless we make a hardware store list, isn't it also likely that we will forget items like virtue and compassion unless we make a character list, or freedom and self-reliance unless we make a citizenship list?"

Our lives are guided by some important lists. And we would do well to review them periodically, particularly when the going gets rough. For example:

All men are created equal.

They are endowed by their creator with certain inalienable rights.

Among these are Life, Liberty and the pursuit of Happiness.

To secure these rights, Governments are instituted among men, deriving their just powers from the consent of the governed.

Whenever any Form of Government becomes destructive of these ends, it is the Right of the People to alter or abolish it, and to institute new Government.

This list, made more than 200 years ago, was the basis of a huge gamble that resulted in the formation of the greatest country the world has known. We have seen these words repeatedly since we were children. But on rereading, they have great power and seem to give new insight each time. Such is the power of a good list. Another example is the Ten Commandments.

Lists are a necessary part of a structured life. Shoppers make lists to be efficient. Pilots use checklists to be thorough and safe. Lists give order to our thinking. Some of the most popular articles we can run in *ColoradoBiz* magazine are lists: Top 250 Public and Private Companies, Readers' Choice Lists, 200 Conference Sites, Top 100 Woman-Owned Companies, Top 100 Minority-Owned Companies, Five Ways to Choose a Good Lawyer, etc.

We bring our best thinking to bear on our problems when we make lists. For example, I'm about to make a list of Five Ways I Can Be a Better Manager. You might want to make your own list before you read mine just to better analyze the process. Our differences will be caused by the different problems we face as managers. If we are honest, the best to-do list that can be made for us is by us. So, here is my list:

Five Ways I Can Be a Better Manager:

- Spend more time listening.
- Give people a better feeling for the big picture.
- See that people get the training they want.
- Make sure that every manager has a replacement coming up.
- Make sure I know the specific goals of every manager that works for me.

Making this list causes us to examine our consciences and come up with things we know, in our hearts, we need to do and are not doing as well as we should. Obviously, our lists will be different. Today's list will be different from next week's because my problems will be different. But if we will work on today's list today, we can put a dent in some problems.

We should make lists for everything if we don't already. And if we are in the habit of making lists, make more.

How about these for starters? (There is, of course, nothing sacred about five.)

- Five Ways to Get to Early Retirement
- Five Ways to Be a Better Father (Mother, Spouse, Neighbor, etc.)
- Five Ways to Live Happier
- Five Ways to Have More Fun
- Five Ways to Be More Fun
- Five Ways to Be a Better Corporate Citizen

Let your natural, problem-solving computer go to work for you. Make a list.

o o o

Getting Promoted

What characteristics disqualify management candidates from moving up?

I was in a discussion recently with a half-dozen managers in the aviation business. We shared ideas on the problems of choosing and promoting people in our departments and businesses.

They all agreed business is good and expanding, and that new and existing managerial positions go unfilled because "It's hard to find good people."

Someone asked the others what they look for in candidates that would disqualify them from the next opportunity. After the obvious answers—doesn't work hard, doesn't understand the business, doesn't play well with others—here are the ones everyone seemed to agree on. Perhaps these thoughts can help you in your career.

Can't see things from management's point of view. Some people who otherwise are deserving never make it to management because they can't seem to stop being the shop steward for the group in which they work. Their solutions to problems never take into account management concerns about the bottom line or productivity. Their suggestions are of this type: "Pay the workers more" and "reduce prices." It's not that these are never good solutions; it's a matter of ongoing attitude.

Has too little respect for others. A spectacular doer who will not give anybody else any credit will not make a very good manager. Often, they are screamers or shouters, and make their point simply by overpowering or belittling. The problem is that no one wants to work for them, and they develop few, if any, good managers themselves.

Always whining. We all know what it's like to work with someone who is perpetually down on the company, always complaining about his or her workload and pay. What a disaster when someone like this becomes a manager. An even more unforgivable infidelity is the whiner who whines outside the company. He or she doesn't deserve a job.

Lacking a sense of humor. Dour managers don't bring out the best in people. And the real challenge of management is to get ordinary people to excel. Generally, we don't give ourselves much credit. So, bringing out the best in people is a tough job, made tougher by someone who takes himself too seriously.

Not willing to commit. It doesn't have to be a commitment forever, but management needs to know the new person on rung one of the management ladder believes in the company and sees a future there for himself or herself. How else could these new managers convince the people who work for them the company is worth the extra effort necessary for excellence?

Fails to understand that after delivering profit today, the primary job of management is to develop the managers who will deliver profit in the future. It's possible our young managers will develop into real leaders despite existing management. But we in existing management fail miserably if we don't provide an atmosphere that nurtures people and brings out the best in them.

If you want to move up to the next level, get a reputation for taking genuine pleasure in the success of others. Encourage, teach, promote and support.

Your Start in Sales Is Not About You

Mr. Big is human, too.

Visiting recently with some excited, energetic new salespeople made me think of my own shaky start in what has become a wonderful career for me.

Almost everyone in selling who is good at it will admit to butterflies (maybe even eagles) at the prospect of making an important presentation to an important person. Or worse, a group of important people. It happens to all of us.

The difference is that the winner gets the presentation done no matter what, and the "not-so-winner" writes a letter instead.

Early in my sales career we lived in Chicago. I can clearly remember driving down Washington Boulevard one morning to call on the purchasing agent of a large company that manufactured timers. As I drove, I had one of those conversations with myself as salesmen often do. I said to myself, "Wiesner, you know more about your product than anybody! This man is going to welcome you with open arms! He's going to call in his engineers for a big meeting and you're going to sell a carload!"

Then another little voice in me said: "You know, Wiesner, these people don't give a rip about you or your product. And you have never really sold a carload or even a big box full! You really don't know what you're going to say. You probably don't know enough to sell them (or anybody) anything."

This internal argument raged all the while I drove to the appointment.

By the time I got to the factory I drove around the block, hoping that I couldn't find a parking place so that I could go back to the office and write a letter! When I actually got to see my "Mr. Big," I was so sure he wouldn't like me or buy my product that I made a meek presentation and left selling nothing.

Three factors were at work keeping me from being successful on this call. First, I spent far too much time thinking of myself, my ability, my knowledge, my experience, how I would look, etc.

The single most dominant factor that robs human beings of self-confidence is self-concern. As salespeople it literally takes our mind off the most important consideration of all: the sales prospect's problem. Our energy (of which we have a finite amount) is expended thinking of our success (or lack of it), of our expertise, rather than thinking genuinely of how we can understand and then solve our prospect's problem. We must get our mind off ourselves and on to the customer's problem we are solving.

Second, I was thinking that "Mr. Big" was some sort of "extra-human being" who was completely out of my class. I suppose it's trite to say "everybody puts their pants on one leg at a time," but it's true! Important people are still people. They probably get where they are because they understand other people. Although they might have built up "masks" and "defenses" because of the deference they are shown, the absolute fact is they will respond to real humanity—real personality—in a positive way. The challenge to us as salespeople is to be genuinely ourselves with "Mr. Big."

Third, I was not comfortable because I had not called on important people very often. In sales, like anything else, there is really no substitute for experience. The people in this world who become what they dream of becoming are not necessarily the people who dream. They are the people who do it, even though it's tough! A good salesperson, hard as it is, goes out of his or her way to develop an ability to call on "important" people. You get better at it, like with a lot of other things, through constant exposure.

That's what "winners" do.

○ ○ ○

Do You Measure Up as a Manager?

Ahh, to see ourselves as others see us! If you can handle it, you could be about to get some good ideas that will help you become the manager you want to be.

Below are a number of characteristics needed by managers and leaders. Read the definitions carefully, then give yourself a grade from 1 to 10, ten being best. After that, for a real test of yourself as a manager, give the test to people on your team, and allow them to respond anonymously.

OK, here goes:

__ Everyone on my team has a clear job description. A person needs to know exactly what is expected of him and how he will be measured.

__ Our group has a set of objectives that every member understands.

__ I have a plan to achieve these objectives that is understood by the entire team. Each member knows his piece of the plan and has had plenty of opportunity to discuss it with me.

__ We train our people to be better. It is good for our company performance, good for company spirit and morale, and good for the individual.

__ I listen. Often. To know the ideas, goals and aspirations of each team member.

__ I am consistent and fair. (If you want a lot of turnover, be the kind of boss nobody can figure out.)

__ I run meetings in which everyone participates. I never just use them as a forum to talk about my ideas. And I respect everyone's time; a one-hour meeting ends in one hour!

__ I never find fault in public, nor do I yell, belittle or insult in private or in public.

__ I give energy. Some managers seem to take something from you every time you deal with them. Be the boss that gives support, enthusiasm, credit and encouragement.

___ I give people jobs that take advantage of their talents and abilities. This draws from them their best possible work and helps them grow.

___ I expect a high level of performance. Everyone who works for me knows exactly what they have to do to get a "job well done."

___ I trust my people, and they know it!

___ I tell each of them often what they are doing right and why I'm glad they are on the team.

___ I talk regularly about things that need improvement, not just at an annual review.

___ I ask what others think and then I listen. I value what others say.

___ I get rid of negative people. It's my job to remove people who don't fit, people who diminish the team.

___ I have a sense of humor. It's only a job and it should be fun.

___ I reward performance. I remember that opportunity and recognition are as important as money.

___ I treat employees like people, not employees. For this I get honesty in return.

In the quiet of your own office, give yourself an honest grade. If your total score is greater than 130, you are very promotable. Under 90, you need a lot of help as a manager. The best way to use this tool about you is to compare your own score with those of anonymous team members. And most importantly, do something about your results when your comparisons are complete.

o o o

The Executive Star

Managers lose, no matter which end of this dynamic they're on.

I knew a publishing executive who lived a remarkable life. He routinely traveled 5,000 or 6,000 miles a week, leaving home on Monday morning and returning late Friday. He often traveled two-thirds of the way across the country just for one meeting, then returned home because he had another meeting the next morning. He was the main man when making customer presentations with his field force. And he did a great job. Nine people reported to him, and everyone looked to him for decisions and direction at home office meetings.

That's also a good description of me in years past. I was busy, frazzled, self-important, independent, tapped out and working mostly alone on a job that required the best work of a lot more people to get it done right. I doubt anyone could have worked harder, yet I was setting myself up for failure.

I was a classic case of a manager who both forced my employees to delegate up and accepted their challenges, making their jobs easier. The net result was a huge load concentrated in one place, with not enough people working on it. Until it catches up with you, it earns you a lot of credit and makes you feel important.

But it's insidiously counterproductive to what a manager is supposed to do. You might have this condition without knowing it. It will make you less effective and perhaps stall your career.

Then there's the manager who asks for problem-solving ideas but whose employees say little, as they're accustomed to this request merely being an introduction to his/her dissertation on the solution. This type of manager often proudly proclaims to be a "workaholic," caused by being indispensable. That limits employees' contributions.

On the other side are those unable to solve problems without your involvement. Try not to let them do it. It's bad for both of your careers.

To be a better manager:

If you're the boss, always ask, "What do you think?" Insist on an answer, listen to it, think about it, try to use it and, in any case, learn to value what your people are saying. Better yet, make them understand their success depends on their contribution.

If you're the boss, don't let any of your people give you the work they should be doing. If the sales manager works for you, don't run the sales meetings. If you make calls with salesmen, don't be the star; let them control the meeting. Let the accounting team lead in producing the budgets, etc. This not only makes your job easier but also builds people—a true manager's highest calling.

If you're the "workaholic" boss, be sure you're doing the work you should be doing and that others are being the contributors they need to be for their own success.

Make a contribution. When your boss asks, deliver. Don't give the problem back without at least suggesting a solution.

Anticipate problems. Come with them solved, or propose a solution.

Don't miss the best parts of life or business. Don't let others delegate up to you; make more time for yourself. Don't let others delegate up to your managers, either.

You'll be a better manager.

How to Find and Keep Good People

He who ignores the growth of his employees will wonder where the customers went.

Good people! We all know that they are the key to having a good or great company. Over the last 25 years we have had our share and managed to keep many of them for a long time.

But we have lost some of the best. It hurt the company and me personally. I always wanted to have the kind of company that would attract and keep good people, yet it didn't always work that way.

Recently, my wife and I stayed in a Hampton Inn hotel. You know the one. They are everywhere—new, clean, pretty good service, convenient, serve a quick breakfast, and they're affordable.

This one was even better! It is in Stuart, Florida, and from the moment we walked in the door until we left the next day, it seemed that every single employee of that place wanted to make sure that we understood that we had spent the night in the most comfortable and friendly hotel ever.

In the morning we had breakfast (you know, the kind where everything comes in, or on, plastic). The food was better than average, and the service a little better yet. A grandmotherly waitress kept coming by with an extra roll or donut and a big grin.

"You look happy!" I said to her.

She smiled big.

"I am!" she said.

"Why?"

"I've been trained!" she said proudly.

I'll bet that everyone working there had been trained to do his or her job well. That made them happy, effective and proud. It also makes for happy customers who will come back.

First, we must help our employees to be the best they can be at their jobs. This means train them and motivate them and then do it again next year. They will be competent and happy, and they will like their customers. Miracles will happen.

For years we didn't do a very good job of training our salespeople. We gave them a list of accounts and a telephone and told them to get their feet wet and come back with problems.

Performance got materially better when we installed a three-day "Rookie Sales Camp" for all new hires. We taught them everything we knew about our business and as much as we could about how to sell our product. It really works.

I've said this before in this column, but I'll say it again because I think it is the most effective way to help people in your organization to grow, to your benefit and theirs:

To help someone grow, help them see themselves in the light of strengths they are unsure of or unaware of, hopefully related to the person they dream of becoming. (I first heard this from Bob James, author and instructor for Dale Carnegie, some 35 years ago.)

To get real results, if you are my boss you must:

1. Find out what or who I dream of becoming; and
2. Help me see and build strengths that will enable me to achieve my most ambitious goals.

If you do this I will give you my best work and my total loyalty.

Good people go through our companies all the time. We just don't recognize them or can't keep them. Companies that keep good people put a lot of effort into helping them become who they want to become.

o o o

Dealing with Problems

When good management is not enough,
leadership is put to the test.

B usiness is tough. The thinnest of margins force projections that will at best produce break-even numbers. Even these, we know, are mostly pie in the sky.

Sales are even tougher, very hard to come by, making foolish scraps of paper out of our hopeful budgets. Competition is fierce, as everyone fights for the business that is there. There is great pressure to cut, reduce and squeeze. Top management and owners want to get more done with fewer people and resources.

Programs start raining down from management. One is called "Break the Bundle." The idea: It is impossible for one person to break a bundle of sticks, but it's easy if each person breaks one stick. Thus, every paper clip and every sheet of copy paper becomes grist for the save-money mill. The product suffers because everyone comes up with a corner cut that lets them claim they are taking care of their "stick."

A boss asks a young manager to make a list of all the people working under him who might be fired or laid-off, should it become necessary. The young manager gets out a piece of paper from a yellow pad, draws a skull and cross bones at the top and begins a list.

Morale is lousy in this environment.

Many would leave, but there is no place to go. Just about every other company is having the same problems. It's hard to sleep at night, and no matter what you do, it doesn't seem to be enough.

Sound familiar? When did all this take place, last week? Actually, in the late '60s. The young manager was me, and I still have the yellow piece of paper with the list I had to make.

So how did it all turn out? Well, I met a leader. Not just a good manager but a real leader from whom I had the good fortune to learn a lot about how to make a business made up of people work. This man—his name is not important so let's call him Vic—had the ability to make everyone who worked for him want to perform well. The reason was simple and basic: You knew that Vic wanted you to be successful. Because his interests included you, you wanted him to be proud of what you did!

We especially need leadership skills when we are trying to grow people, survive tough times, get extraordinary work out of ordinary people and provide a track for future leaders. To paraphrase Sir H.G. Selfridge, London department store magnate:

- The manager drives the people; the leader coaches.
- The manager depends on authority; the leader on goodwill.
- The manager says "I"; the leader says "We."
- The manager fixes blame; the leader fixes the problem.
- The manager knows; the leader shows.
- The manager says "Go"; the leader says "Let's Go!"

These are times when business is starved for leadership.

Get Busy. It's the First Day of the Rest of Your Life!

Is it possible to catch up after messing up?

A high-school junior, the daughter of a 30-year friend of the family, called me and asked if I would answer a few questions about what it takes to be successful in business for an article she was doing for the school paper.

I was flattered and told her I'd be glad to help.

While she was framing her first question, I relaxed, ready to pontificate a bit on business success.

I immediately sat straight up in my chair at her first question. It went like this: "There's a lot of pressure in our school to get a 4.0, but my mom says that you said you never did well in school and yet you did well in business. She says that you told her that usually the A+'s from school end up working for the C's in the real world. Is that how it works?"

Trapped! What do I tell her? The facts were that I did not do very well in school, at least for most of it. It wasn't until I was a junior in college when the dean of students came to me and said that if I didn't change my work habits I would not graduate. At that late stage of the game, something clicked in me, and I did change—and I even made the dean's list that year and the next. But I really was a late starter. No 4.0 for me.

I don't know if I'll ever say it again, but I have been known to say something like that business about the A's working for the C's.

How do I explain that to study is good? How do I excuse being able to run a business after blowing high school?

So we talked for a while and pretty much decided that we agreed on these ideas:

Different people wake up at different times in their lives. Some "get it" in time to make a 4.0 in high school. Some don't wake up until much later. Some never do. You will know that you "get it" when you find yourself saying, "This is the first day of the rest of my life; get busy!"

Of course, it becomes harder and harder to make something happen the older you are when you decide to do it. My hat is off to those who get out in the workforce, get married, have kids and then decide to go back to school. When these people get it done, they really accomplish something.

The most important things to bring to a job are the ability to read and interpret, to write and express yourself, to think, a positive attitude and a good work ethic. The rest will come. This is true after high school or in mid-career. Of course, doctoring or lawyering or business requires a specific body of knowledge. If you don't get started on this early, odds are you will never get it. So get started.

The principle of "what have you done lately?" is always at work. When you are 35 years old, your high school 4.0 is of little importance compared with what you have been doing in your career. But when you graduate high school, you have nothing to show except your grades.

A couple of points we didn't discuss that I wish we had: First, we let bridges burn when we are young. For example, I think I would have made a good doctor, but every year that I sat by and watched myself accomplish nothing, another bridge to being a doctor burned, eliminating the possibility. There is a lot to be said for coming from behind to be a writer and publisher, etc., but why not preserve all our options while we are young?

Second, we will have these thoughts for as long as we care about our career. So get busy. This is the first day of the rest of our lives!

Free Beer Tomorrow!

Deal with it now or pay the price later.

There are at least two great restaurants in Sedalia, Colorado. You probably know about Gabriel's, the fancy bistro in a beautiful old Sedalia house where the waiters are dressed to the nines, and you had better be, too. It's well worth the trip because the food and service are spectacular, while the wine selection and ambiance are second to none in Colorado. It's a great place for a special occasion, but you might not know about the great restaurant right across Sedalia's main drag.

Bud's Cafe and Bar is the kind of place you used to find in the neighborhoods of Chicago or Milwaukee. Bud's has only one menu item—hamburgers You can get 'em regular or double, with or without cheese. Don't ask for fries—they don't serve them— but the hamburgers you should try. One of the things I like best about Bud's is the sign that proclaims "Free Beer Tomorrow!" When my 22-year-old son first saw it, he eagerly started planning his activities for the following day, until he came to a realization when he arrived the next day that the sign would still promise the same thing.

I love the irony of the sign, because it reminds me of the many times I have been seduced by the comforting thought that tomorrow will bring a fix to all my problems; that today, I could just relax. I can't help but think of all the money it cost me to put off sales calls until "tomorrow," the employees I've messed up by not dealing with people problems immediately and the accumulated effects of putting off decisions simply because they were tough.

If we were to sit down and make a list of the qualities we would like to find in our employees, certainly the list would include characteristics that define a doer, not a procrastinator. But we only get what we deserve.

As managers, we have to set up a system that is a sign in the window that hopefully makes everyone a "today" person. rather than a "tomorrow" person.

People will adjust to their environment. And I have some thoughts on making that environment one where employees see that facing up to the hard work today is rewarded:

Be the kind of manager who provides the template. When you say, "I'll call you this afternoon with the answer," do it. Expect everyone in your department to do the same. Don't leave any doubt about your own ability to do what you ask of others.

When faced with a difficult people decision, handle it then. For example, whenever I've put off firing someone who I knew didn't belong in their job—because I was waiting for the situation to improve—I've made a mistake. When someone really doesn't belong, it's been bad for business, bad for morale and even worse for the person. As soon as you're sure, do something.

Almost everybody hates paperwork. If the bosses joke about it and don't take it seriously, everyone else will, too. Set up a discipline that starts at the top and is expected throughout the entire group.

Everyone will feel more organized, have more time for core work (selling, accounting, etc.), and morale will be positively affected.

We all want employees who will do things now. We won't have any unless we are the same way.

The truth is, free beer tomorrow always costs more than it does today.

o o o

Want to Pick Up a Step or Two on Your Competition?

Write stronger letters.

There is really no such thing as a bad letter because they all are communication. But there are strong letters and there are weak letters. For example, this is a weak letter:

Dear Mr. Big,

I would like to introduce myself and my product. I know that you are a very busy man and so I'll endeavor to be brief. I'm sure that you would like to increase production without increasing costs, thus increasing your profit.

As per the attached brochure please be apprised that our product blah, blah, blah ... rest of three-page sales letter.

We can probably make a living sending letters like this, but if you and I want to earn a good living, there are ways to do it better. Here are some suggestions for improving the above letter.

Limit the I, me, we, ours. Look at the letters that come to your desk. Better yet, look at the letters you and your people are sending. We should all have a rule that no letter that starts with "I" shall ever leave our office! The "you, your" words should outnumber the "I, me" words at least four to one.

Don't sound like a doormat. "You are busy" implies that I am not. "I'll be brief" implies that what you have to say is not all that important. We do the same thing on the phone: "Thank you for taking my call. I know that you are very busy; I'll be brief." Sounds to me like he probably shouldn't have taken the call after all. Just eliminate these phrases from your writing and selling.

Be appropriately brief. The most powerful sales letters are on one side of one sheet of paper. What was the last great four-pager you remember? Every time I come up with a situation I think is an exception, someone shows me how to do it easier and shorter.

Don't try to get too much into one letter. It's really hard to get across a six-point program in a letter. Better to use the letter to get an appointment. Or send a series of letters. Or send an attachment with the letter, where the letter is written to generate the necessary interest in reading the attachment.

Try to be different. Remember how many of our competitors are writing to our clients and realize that we might make a living writing and sounding like all the rest, but if we want to make a great living we should find a way to be distinctive. Of course we must still be ourselves. If we paste on some foreign personality, we will be phony and everyone will know it.

Write the way you talk. Why is it that when we write we use words like "pursuant," "endeavor" and "attached" and phrases like "per our previous"— words that we would never use in normal conversation. If we want to come through the written words as competent, friendly and comfortable, we've got to use the same words we would use in conversation. When you finish a letter, reread it and give it a grade for "Is this really me?" Don't send the letter until it gets an "A."

Write friendly. Don't make the type small in order to cram more into the letter. Try writing letters that don't use block paragraphs and do indent. They read more friendly.

This would be my first try at improving the earlier letter:

Dear Mr. Big,

You are probably very proud of the notice your company is getting in the news these days. It was nice to read of your success in the WSJ. (Whatever you say here has to be true and the result of some effort at research on your part.)

Did you know that some companies in your industry have used our product so they can be more competitive? (What you say here must be interesting and make him want to hear more.)

I've included some additional explanation but I'd really like to ... (Here ask for the kind of appointment or phone meeting or even the actual order.) I'll follow up by ....

So, what are your ideas?

○ ○ ○

Making It in Management

Some do, some don't. Why?

Many years ago, I got my first job in management the way many salespeople do: I sold more advertising than anyone else, and the management at my company at the time thought that was the key to discovering new management talent. I was given the P&Ls for the last three years and told that I would be expected to be up to speed by the next monthly management meeting. That was pretty much the extent of my training, probably the rough equivalent of whatever else passed as management training then (in the late '60s) and now.

What I learned from my "training" was that numbers were more important than anything else. Sales numbers, profit numbers, cost figures, etc. Management presided over these numbers and managed what made them go up and down. I traveled a lot, and when I saw customers with our local sales guys, I would help them by sort of taking over like some kind of "super-salesman." I suppose the local salesman was happy when we were successful, but it didn't do much for his self-confidence. At the same time, I worked the numbers so that we would have money left over and be profitable.

I wasn't really a very good manager because I was stuck on managing things.

It wouldn't be until two jobs (and accompanying mediocre performances) later that I began to see that really good managers spend as much time with people as they do with things. You can't ignore things and be a great manager, but neither can you ignore people and be a great manager.

So, here's how to make it as a manager:

Managing is a lot more than scorekeeping. A friend of mine once characterized his rapid rise in the corporate structure as starting as a player (salesman), moving to coach (sales manager) and then to scorekeeper (management). If you are in a management job that makes you primarily a scorekeeper, change your job or change your employer.

Any plan for a manager that doesn't include a plan to make the people you manage successful has little chance for more than average success, if that.

Have a good plan for your group and make sure that everybody knows it. If we are to march up the hill for you, we have to know what's at the top, why it is important and what we will get for our group and ourselves if we are successful. The more you include us in the decision process and make us feel like we helped formulate the goal, the tougher team we will be.

Let every individual see his or her own strengths that will enable each to achieve. The real key to leadership is being able to motivate people, because you know what they are individually trying to accomplish and are helping them do it through the team goal. This is a lot easier to say than it is to do. Remember, the most valuable manager is the one who truly enjoys the success of the people he or she manages.

Attitude. Everyone will admit that a positive attitude makes for a great leader and manager, and such a person is fun to work for and will get a lot done. Well, everyone is right. Be a "Yes sir, we can do that!" kind of person and make your group feel that way, too.

Bring ideas, plans and solutions. Business, and everything else for that matter, is full of problems, negativism, hand-wringing and complaints. Be just the opposite. Never bring a problem or complaint unless you have a solution to suggest.

Bottom line: We manage things and lead people. Leaders make it in management because they think about the people.

o o o

Out of Africa

There is no place like home, a fact easily rediscovered upon returning from any foreign country.

It was the trip of a lifetime. For years we had talked about taking a vacation in Africa. We planned it for months, and a few weeks ago we left excited and expectant. We weren't disappointed.

As for the animals, it's like being in the zoo. Not at the zoo, but in it. To illustrate the amount of wildlife: In a chunk of the African bush about the size of South Park, Colorado, put 50 lions, 30 elephants, some hippos, rhinos, 10,000 antelope, thousands of buffalo and all sorts of smaller game. Then pitch a canvas tent in the middle of it! It is impossible to put into words the excitement of being just a few feet away from these dangerous denizens, with neither bars nor barricades. (We have hundreds of pictures.)

Geographically, it's like nothing we had seen. Not only is it huge, but it also is dotted with wonders of the world, like Victoria Falls (twice the height of Niagara Falls and home of the world's highest bungee jump off the bridge over the Zambezi), the confluence of the Atlantic and Indian Oceans at the Cape of Good Hope, and the Okevunga Delta, where a huge river disappears into the desert. People have spent their lives exploring this fascinating continent.

The social problems would confound a thousand Solomons. For example, Zimbabwe has three million citizens, including 50,000 whites. About 1,500 whites own all the available land. In Botswana, there are 50,000 excess elephants (very destructive animals) while rhinos are almost extinct because the Chinese place such high value on the aphrodisiac qualities of their horns. In both countries, the native blacks are being pushed off the land that was theirs for generations to save animals that draw tourists.

What a trip! So exciting, so interesting!

But it happened to me again. Returning to this country, I experienced strong feelings that are hard to explain. A mixture of security, belonging and hope, and for some reason, I was nearly bursting with pride. Even with everything that needs fixing here, we have the best in the world.

Those who think this is such a bad place to live should visit South Africa. In Johannesburg, I was told, they have 10 carjackings each day, and more often than not, they take your car and your life. South Africa has six black tribes that have been trying to eradicate each other for centuries, and they won't stop trying. It's the African counterpart to Bosnia-Herzegovina. Their fathers hated each other, their sons hate each other and their grandsons will try to wipe out each other.

We don't have the most perfect of societies, but sometimes we forget what we have in the United States is so much better than what exists in almost every other part of the world. We certainly are not finished yet, but we have made more progress on human rights and for minorities than anywhere. We have the freest press in the world. There are few countries where you can criticize the government like you can here.

But *opportunity* is our biggest asset, the envy of every country I have visited. It abounds here like nowhere else.

Here, at home.

Living through Hard Times

From people who have lived through them before.

The boss called me in and began to outline for me just how bad things were. Instead of the gains we had been projecting, we were now expecting to have a decline of at least 15 percent for the upcoming year unless something really good and unexpected happened. By the end of the week I was to have a list of people who would be considered for layoffs.

I went to my office and made a list of all the people working for me. I made it in inverse order, with my name at the top as the last to go, down to the bottom, which was the name of the first to be laid off. This happened in 1967. We actually got through about 15 percent of the list before things got better.

In the '80s in Denver, things were just as tough.

A commercial real estate broker told me then that his 5-year-old son had asked, "Daddy, what's a crane?" And it dawned on my friend that his son, the son of a broker of buildings, had never seen a construction crane, because in the previous four years, no buildings had been built in Denver.

This will be, if memory serves, my fourth recession since entering the workforce.

We were well on the way to having this one when the terrorist attacks brought it to us faster. And they are probably making it deeper.

Trying to get a bearing on things, I've been asking many "old" guys like myself just what advice they would give about surviving the downturn. Some thoughts for companies:

AT THE TOP

This difficult period will end. Most experts say we will begin to recover in six to 12 months. The main responsibility of management is to see that the company comes out of the recession healthy. Healthy means with a business, with a team and with cash.

This point should be made again. Running out of cash is the worst kind of disaster. Everyone in the company is depending on you to manage this well.

Good managers will decide how to "cut the cloth to fit the suit," and then be aggressive in maintaining business. If people cuts must be made, be fair and respectful and remember that management is at least part of the reason cuts must be made. Do everything you can to help people who have been laid off.

Help the team succeed. Measure success with indexes that work even in bad times. For example, use share of market instead of growth to define sales success.

People will survive even pay cuts if there is some other way to feel that they are contributing and making a positive difference.

EVERYBODY

Now is not the time for standing around the coffee machine with whiners. Now is the time to stand out because of hard work and positive attitude. Decide that you and your company are both going to advance a rung or two on the ladder so when business improves you'll be set for growth.

Like always, everyone will know who has his or her shoulder to the wheel and who does not. If we demonstrate leadership now, it will follow us when better times return.

Keep things in perspective, particularly if you have lost your job. Six percent unemployment is still 94 percent employment; things are returning to normal, and we are making progress against terrorism.

Don't forget to be a leader for family and friends. Feedback from that will make you stronger at work. If you are out of work, you will draw strength from your family and be back at a job sooner than you think.

What it comes down to: Work harder than ever, manage resources wisely and help everyone do better.

Don't worry about the future; work to ensure that it gets better. Remember: More recessions are on the way, and we should learn what we can from this one.

o o o

A Bad Day

Our frame of mind determines how we deal with everyday life. Is it any wonder that young people form gangs and work out their frustrations in ways that give them lifelong problems?

The guy pulled right up behind me, within six inches of my back bumper, it seemed. We were both doing sixty or sixty-five. He flashed me his brights, assuming I'd be obedient and pull over.

I was driving home in the outside lane of E-470, and the traffic was really thick. I was on my cellular phone, trying to tie up one last loose-end in the day of endless loose ends. It had been almost a record-breaking, all-time lousy day: A competitor was slashing prices and swiping business, I had offended some really good people in our company, the dog was sick, the kid's report card was bad and my new mutual fund had taken a nose-dive. It was one of those days when I felt incompetent, unlucky, frustrated and testy.

And now I had this clown on my tail, trying to blink me over.

I've always had a pet peeve about drivers who follow too closely at high speed. I've lectured my kids when they were learning to drive about allowing "10 feet for every 10 mph," and so forth.

This guy behind me was the last straw. I was going the speed limit or better and he had muscled into my space. I wasn't going to move. My whole day focused into this one instant, and I touched the brake, delighted that his whole field of vision would be filled with red light from my brakes. Having responded appropriately to his flashing lights, I drove on—in the left lane.

He went ballistic. I saw in my mirror that he and his passenger were waving, gesturing and mouthing what could only be blistering invective. I had a momentary burst of victory. He then pulled into the right lane and accelerated, still gesturing wildly and mouthing unheard curses. He pulled even and veered toward me as he passed, trying to run me off the road. By the time I pulled back onto the road from the shoulder, he had passed, breaking off the skirmish with a one-finger salute.

No way! I growled an invective of my own and smashed the accelerator to the floor to give chase.

Something made me stop and ask, "Whoa, Wiesner, what are you doing here?" Did I really want to hit this man's car? Or have a fistfight at the side of the road? Or what? I felt stupid. Really stupid. I felt I had been sucked into some game that I didn't want any part of. Then, I began to feel lucky. This could have ended in so many bad ways.

Many times since this incident, I have thought about how tension and frustration—especially frustration—turn into anger and rage that act as catalysts for stupid behavior. If I, a person with everything going for me, can get so frustrated, what about the person whose life is a daily hourly struggle?

I believe that young people, particularly young minority people, are frustrated by what they see as their opportunities. Often, the system offers them little hope for a reasonable future. Many of these people carry 10 times the psychological load of "majority" adults, and some make mistakes dealing with it. It seems to me the chief cause for frustration for young adults today is not being able to see a place for themselves in the system.

I have a suggestion. Let's all make it our business to give some hope to a young person who may not see his/her place in the system. Take an intern or two from the local high school. Perhaps being a Big Brother or Sister is your way. Or be a mentor for the Colorado Business Alliance for Youth. Don't be discouraged that you can only tackle the problem in ones or twos. There are enough of us to help lots of young people out there who need guidance around life's minefields of frustration.

I don't blast down the left lane any more. This is a much better way to live.

o o o

What Makes an Exceptional Boss?

Everybody remembers the best one or two bosses they ever had. What do you and I need to do to be thought of as one of the best?

R ecently, I have received a flurry of letters that often sound like this: "For months I have been trying to understand what has happened to my motivation and drive at work. I have been this company's top sales performer for several years, driven and motivated by my own success, or so I thought. I have come to believe my sales manager is an important part of my motivation. The problem is, my new sales manager is a very strong believer in himself, not necessarily in his sales team."

When someone says, "I've got a lousy boss!" listeners usually nod in understanding, because we have all been there and somehow comprehend without much explanation.

But when someone announces they have a great boss, we want to know why.

What makes your boss so great? Is he or she doing something that I can do also?

It begins with the concept of "boss" as opposed to manager or leader. There are managers who become so absorbed managing things, like numbers and call sheets, that they totally miss the human part of the equation. Conversely, there are leaders who are so charismatic that we charge up their hill, only to find nothing at the top of the hill. The leader's plan was bad, and we have misspent our faith.

A real "boss" brings the best of both worlds.

A real "boss" will be very clear on the following four points:

A workable plan. The goal will be exciting. The payoff, if we accomplish the goal, will be worth our hard effort. The plan will be painstakingly thought out. It will be carefully and completely communicated to everyone who will have a part in its success. Everyone involved will have a chance for input and buy-in. It becomes workable when everyone with a part to play thinks it will work and wants it to work.

A team. A great boss will pick a team with whom I am proud to work.

People who inspire and contribute and who make me want to inspire and contribute. A great team will coalesce only around the kind of boss that takes more obvious pleasure in the success of the team and each of its members individually than in his/her own success. There can be no great team without an unselfish boss. It's a lucky person who gets to work once in a career on such a team.

A job that fits each team member. We all need a job that we can do but that stretches us. We need to know how the job fits into the whole. Nothing is so confusing and uninspiring as a "chore" for which we don't know the purpose or intent. Our job needs to be tough enough so that we will feel good when it's accomplished. We need very much to hear our successes publicly celebrated.

A great boss will have a personal interest in my success. This will be visceral and critical. Going back to the letter at the top of the page, if you and I as bosses don't signal clearly to those we boss that we are as interested in their success as we are in our own, we will lose good people, and in the end we will simply be stymied in business.

Good bosses are defined by the people who work for them, not by themselves. If you are not a good boss, you don't deserve to advance in your company.

○ ○ ○

Do it Like Tito Puente

Leadership lessons from a Latin jazz great

This winter while spending some time in Florida, my wife and I went to a show put on by Tito Puente, Jr. She said she bought tickets because Puente is a guitar player and I have been taking guitar lessons. (Turns out he is mainly a drummer, but we had a wonderful time anyway.)

His father was also Tito Puente, who I remembered from the late '50s and '60s as a great salsa musician. The son saluted the father with love and respect many times during the evening.

The Lyric Theater in Stuart, Florida held five hundred to six hundred people. We probably got the last tickets to be had, and were seated up in the balcony just a few feet from the ceiling.

Puente's band had three trumpets, a sax, a guitar, a base, a piano, two guys on bongos, and probably a couple more I can't remember. And of course, Puente himself was on the drums.

For more than an hour, the decibel level in that old hall was in the stratosphere. The people in the seats couldn't keep still ... they were jumping, twisting and writhing, whether sitting or standing.

There wasn't a bad seat in the house. Each of the band members had a solo or two, some had more, and Puente cheered them on mightily.

The piano and the horns were sensational. The bongo players made those little drums talk, and the crowd went crazy. And all the while, Puente—in a full suit and tie—wailed on the drums with what, at times, seemed like four or five sticks. The band had to be wearing down as the crowd got wilder.

What really got me was the big finish. Puente took off his suit jacket, got a towel and wiped his face.

As he stepped away from center stage and his drum setup, he invited one of the bongo players to sit at the maestro's drums. The bongo player stepped into Puente's territory, picked up his sticks and began to play.

His sound was different than Puente's, but at least as good, if not better. Puente was swinging his towel in the air, leading cheers for the drummer, and the crowd loved it.

Then he did it again. Puente got the other bongo player to move over to his drums and play. The same thing happened, only it was better. The crowd amped up again, and Puente encouraged their roars.

The band members all went back to their normal places and played one more, each featured one last time. The crowd was entertained, the band had a ball, and everybody was happy.

And I think Puente was pleased. Why? Because he seemed to understand that a leader's job is not to be better than everyone on the team, but to bring out the best in each team member and thus make each successful. He is good enough to have the top spot in any salsa band, but if he couldn't build a team, he would be traveling as a one-man show.

Going to that concert reminded me of a basic leadership principle: Leaders are good at building people and teams, not at climbing to the top over others.

So, what now? How does one go about building people up? Here are some ideas:

- Spend quality time and get to know your people well enough to get honest answers to questions like: What are your long and short-term goals?
- Exchange your aspirations for theirs. Something like: I will help you where I can if you will help me achieve my goals with this team.
- Exchange ideas often to uncover how things are going for both parties. Ask: How am I doing? After listening to the answer, ask the same question of him/her.
- Do like Puente—Help each team/band member look good. Challenge them.
- Make a pact of "No surprises." Don't forget important details, like: We are hiring a new person at your level. And you will not surprise me by not telling me about, say, a missed sales target or a problem employee. You will be happy to discover how comfortable a "No surprises" agreement makes everyone feel.

Finally, just enjoy the music of a team working together in harmony.

o o o

Selling Is Easy

At least, good salespeople can make it look that way.

The way I remember this story may not be as accurate in the details as I would like, but it is essentially correct. And it makes the most fundamental truths of the sales process seem much clearer because it is a true story.

Years ago, like 25 or 30, a gifted man named Fred Herman appeared on the Johnny Carson Show. The Carson Show, as many know, was what we used to watch before Jay Leno and Dave Letterman. Fred Herman was a world-renowned sales personality who went around the country giving presentations to groups on selling. Fred was the best. In his day there was no better trainer, no better speaker.

The encounter went something like this: Carson was a smoker and would often smoke while he was interviewing guests. He said to Fred, "You're supposed to be such a good salesman, sell me something!" And he began to look around his desk for something to make Fred sell as an example. Of course, he had an ashtray right in front of him and pushed it over to Fred and said, "If you're so good, sell me this ashtray!"

Herman picked it up and held it in front of him as if he owned it. He said to Carson, "Are you enjoying smoking that cigarette?"

"Yeah," replied Carson.

"It looks like you've smoked up lots of ashes there; what do you plan to do with 'em?"

Looking at the possessive grip that Herman had on the ashtray, Carson said, "Right now I'm not so sure."

"Well," said Fred victoriously, "I have here an ashtray. Would you like to buy it?" And everybody in the studio, Carson and Herman included, joined in great laughter.

What Fred had done was a perfect example of what the sales process should be. It wasn't long, involved or wordy. He didn't launch into a recitation of all the reasons why someone would want to buy an ashtray. He found the one that was of crucial interest to Carson and used only that. He did it using questions. No claims, no brag, no promises—just a simple question that made it clear to his prospect that he really needed this product.

There are two points to make here that embrace almost the entire body of knowledge necessary to be a successful salesman. (It's embarrassing that this profession is so easily mastered!) First, the power of questions. The way a good salesman uses questions makes them hundreds of times more effective than statements. Consider the difference between "This ashtray is designed to hold ashes" and "What do you plan to do with those ashes?" The statement is feeble when it comes to getting information from the prospect. The question requires an answer, and the answer will tell you just what the prospect is thinking!

The question makes the prospect picture himself enjoying the use of the product.

To become better at selling, to make more money and be more fulfilled in our jobs, we should constantly be developing our ability to ask questions that count.

The second point is that Fred used the simplest, yet most complete, formula for a sale that is possible:

Ask a question .... Wait for an answer .... Make a statement. Ask for the order.

"You got an ash problem?" .... "Yeah" .... "I got a solution!" "Want to buy my ashtray?"

Try it!

o o o

Breakfast of Champions

Successful people, in sports or in business, make it seem so simple. How do they do it?

I recently attended the annual Denver "Dinner of Champions," an event that honored local businesspeople who had done a lot in the fight against muscular dystrophy (specifically in this case: Bob Malone, chairman of Western Capital, and his wife, Kalleen). As part of the proceedings they introduced four athletes who had accomplished a lot. There was marathon winner Frank Shorter, speed skater Ann Henning Walker, Olympic skier Bill Johnson and football player and coach Raymond Berry.

What they did then was unusual—at least, I had never seen it done before. The four were simply given microphones and from the podium, sitting in deck chairs, they all answered the question "What does it take to be a champion?" None of them had any notes, and it appeared that they were each thinking through their answer for the first time.

Each of these people, at the very top of their respective fields, started their answer with "You've got to have a goal!"

Skier Johnson recalled that he knew when he was eight years old that he would one day be the best in the world, he just didn't realize during which specific Winter Olympics. Skater Walker talked of being so impressed with an Olympic medal winner she met when she was a youngster that she promised herself she would do the same thing one day.

Marathoner Shorter spoke of hard work and trust in oneself, and of having the true belief that "I can do it!" Coach Berry talked of the extra measure of inner strength that comes from a team, associates and family.

But all came back to the simple ideas of (a) have a goal; know exactly and specifically what you want to accomplish, and (b) make sure that each and every day you do something to accomplish that goal.

In business everyone would admit that nothing is more important than an objective, but how many of us are right this minute operating without a practical plan to achieve our goal, one that makes us perform?

If success in your sales job requires 100 sales per year and it takes eight appointments to get a sale and four phone calls to get an appointment, you will fail if you don't make at least 16 phone calls and more than three face-to-face appointments every day.

If your goal is to break into management and you don't do something every day in the job you have right now to promote harmony and enthusiastic cooperation and to help your co-workers be successful, you will probably never make it.

If you want to be the best writer in town and you don't make yourself write some of your best stuff every day, forget it.

I know a publisher of the number-two trade magazine in a certain industry. This person's goal is to be number one. Every business decision on this magazine is put to the test of "Is this what the number-one magazine would do?" (For example, Would the number-one publication exhibit at this show? How would the number-one magazine present this story?) In my opinion, by holding up these standards for themselves every day, this magazine will become number one.

Every day, breakfast for real champions in sports or business or wherever has to include serious reflection on how this particular day will bring them closer to their goals.

The Seven Deadly Sins of Management

Some things managers do make them nonmanagers, whether or not they get away with them.

Books and articles are full of things we must do to be good leaders and managers. So, I thought it would be interesting to list things from the other point of view.

These are at the top of my list of things not to do. Unless I really need the job, I will not work for you for long (at the least, I will not give you my best) if you:

Have all the ideas. It seems everyone has worked for someone who never really accepts an idea that comes from someone else in the group. The latest idea always needs to be reworked, usually by the boss. It becomes acceptable when it gets his or her imprint on it.

The effective leader draws ideas from others in his group in an atmosphere of encouragement and acceptance. If you can't get good ideas from your group, look to yourself, not at group members.

Take all the credit. It usually is easy to spot this kind of manager. He or she uses words like "I", "me," "my group," "my people"—you get the idea. He or she is always a little condescending toward the others involved and never willing to give any credit.

An effective leader is anxious to spread the credit to group members. He/she realizes the only way a manager can be successful is if his/her people are successful.

Don't pay me what I'm worth. We all know when we are being unfairly dealt with. I may need this job, so I won't tell you what I really think. But if I ever get a chance to leave, I will. In the meantime, realize that much of my creative energy is spent imagining myself working elsewhere.

Make me do all the work. Just about everyone that works for us has a lot more to give than we get. For you to get my hardest effort, I have to feel we're in this together. Try to outwork me. If I'm the right person for the job, I'll keep up. Perhaps I'll carry more than my share, happily too, if you get the rest of this list right.

Treat me like a mushroom. You know the old joke about being treated like a mushroom, kept in the dark and fed a bunch of horse--. Some managers think they are the only ones who deserve to fully understand the problem at hand.

If you want to get my best work, treat me like an important equal, at least an important part of the equation. Tell me your goals; let me in on the secret. Let me see my place in the solution to the problem. Help me see how my future improves because I am a contributor. Treat me like an insider and I will treat you like a real leader.

Criticize me in any public forum. Some so-called managers gain self-worth by taking it from others. I'm no different than you. My self-respect is fragile. I can take criticism. I actually want it in the right form. But if you belittle me in public or in private, you will lose me forever as a supporter.

An exceptional manager helps his/her people learn. When criticism is needed, it is given. In private. And in a way that recognizes the overall worth of the person. I will benefit and try harder if you do it right.

Block me from your bosses. Why do some managers think it is important to shield top management from the rest of the workers? It's as if they don't want to risk someone else getting credit.

If you are proud of me, you will want me to spend time with your management. I'll make you look good because I know your success is my success.

Block me from my future. Some managers seem to fear growth of their employees. It's as if they seek success by climbing on the backs of their people, absorbing their upward energy in the process.

I will give you my best work if I see you are interested in me achieving my personal goals. I will want you to achieve your goals if, in doing so, you will help me get to mine.

OK, that's eight. So, I can't count. You probably have at least seven more. Send 'em; we'll print 'em.

o o o

A Manager Worth Working For

How do you know when you've found the right manager
to throw in with?

There was Fred, Paul, Boo, John, Stan, Larry, Jerry, Terry and Mr. Benion, just to mention the ones that come immediately to mind.

Those people are bosses I have had over the years. Mr. Benion was one of the first. He owned the drugstore in Buffalo, N.Y., where I held my first real job besides a paper route. I was a soda jerk behind a fountain, making and serving shakes and hamburgers.

But only a couple of these guys were really worth working for.

By being "worth it" I mean they either turned me on to their plan, helped me learn something or taught me something about life or success.

For example, Mr. Benion didn't talk to me very much. When he closed the lunch counter in his pharmacy, all he told me was that I didn't have a job anymore. I had no idea whether I was part of the problem or part of the solution.

If you're the boss, you have to get me to buy into a worthwhile goal, and have an organized plan to get it accomplished. Without those two ingredients, you will have little chance of keeping top producers on your team.

A few really good bosses that I've had, however, had some things in common. Here are four characteristics of successful bosses that you don't find in everyone. They can make the difference between an exciting, rewarding job and one that has you looking for reasons to play golf instead of work.

A great boss makes me feel important if not critical to success. If you're the boss and I'm the worker, you have to spend the time necessary to explain and bring me in on your plan as a key player. Your plan will be aggressive and exciting. You will have to convince me not only that I am essential to achieving the goal but also that I have what it takes to get the job done. To a large extent, my confidence is your responsibility.

A great boss is a builder of people. If you're the boss, I will think that you get a bigger kick out of my success than you do from your own. I will be convinced that you are truly interested in my success, in my achieving whatever it is that I consider important. You will have spent considerable time with me to get to know what makes me tick and what my goals are. You will be a believer in training and education, and you will see to it that I get all I need to be the best in my field. You will have found a way to roll up my goals into yours. If I am successful, we will both be successful.

A great boss knows the difference between "managing" and "leading." If you are the boss, you know that we manage "things" and lead "people." You manage meetings, calendars, production schedules, rate sheets, etc. A great boss leads people by putting it all together so that everyone gets it. You have a great plan, sell it to great people, create a team by giving everyone a stake and showing them how they will get closer to their personal goals through team success.

A great boss will help you keep your life balanced. If you are the boss, you will make it clear that education and family are every bit as important as a job. If someone uses all their energy on the "job" it's likely they won't last, much less have a successful life in the greater sense.

If you find someone who thinks like this, throw in with them. It will be fun, educational and rewarding.

o o o

Thoughts from the Genghis Khan School of Management

A little tough at times, but a great leader and instinctive manager of people.

Genghis Khan was the greatest conqueror of all time, measured by the land mass he controlled. His empire at its peak was more than five million square miles, more than twice that of Alexander the Great and five times that of Hitler. He had more than 700 tribes and cities under his rule, and his domain stretched from the Caspian Sea to the Sea of Japan.

The Great Khan (as he was called by his people) managed to capture in only 25 years more land than the Romans had conquered in more than 400 years.

I came across these facts and wondered how a man on horseback armed with a bow and arrows could possibly solve the management problems built into such an accomplishment.

Management problems like: With an army of 50,000, how do you discuss strategy? How do you give orders when the only communication device you have is the unaided human voice? When another tribe was conquered in battle, how did he manage these "mergers"? How did he keep peace between all these fierce warriors from all the incompatible Mongol tribes of the Eurasian steppes (another word for grassy plains)? As his "company" grew, how did he "manage" the diversity of interest and loyalty and keep his growing forces focused?

In the last couple of months I have read a couple of books (*Genghis: Birth of an Empire* and *Genghis: Lords of the Bow*, both by Conn Iggulden) and watched a movie (*Mongol*) about the Great Khan. I also have read a lot from Googling.

The first thing to deal with is his reputation for savagery. The idea that he could keep everyone in his growing army in line by merely killing anyone who stepped out of line was foolish. These other Mongolians were just as savage if not more so than Khan. Threatening them with death would have provoked nothing more than a big fight and the breaking up of Khan's army. Although Khan had his rules—i.e., you would die quickly if you cheated him, lied to him, attacked his family, stole his wife (one sorry Mongol did just that and his entire clan was put to death) or refused allegiance after being conquered—he was generally a pretty even-handed and fair ruler.

After conquering a country, Genghis Khan asked every man to individually swear loyalty to him. He would then guarantee them security and food and usually leave the same people in control as were in control before the "merger."

Khan never tried to change the religious beliefs of the "merged." Interestingly, at approximately the same time, the Christians were in their second crusade to insist that everyone become Christian.

Genghis Khan was the first to consider "span of control," although there is no evidence that he called it that.

It was then and still is the answer to the question "How many people can a person effectively manage?" He organized his army with a system of 10. Ten men to a squad, 10 squads to a company, 10 companies to a division and 10 divisions to a "lumen." Everyone in his army trained every day. Everyone knew his job and its relationship with everyone else's job when the day for battle came.

Khan believed that "he who exalts himself should be humbled," and he had a reputation for crushing the self-important. At the same time, he took care of teachers, doctors and engineers, whom he never taxed.

He introduced a writing system (still in use today) to communicate with people not standing in front of him, a postal service to deliver his communiqués, and was the first to introduce paper money. Not bad for a ferocious Mongol.

For amazing results à la the Great Khan:

Keep only the best people.
Look after their needs.
Organize so that no one is in the dark.
Train, train, train.
Go after it hard!

o o o

Exporting Our Expertise

The real future of the underdeveloped countries of the world lies in our ability to get good old-fashioned American business principles of honesty, integrity and profit into their business systems.

In a few weeks, Janusz is coming to visit. Janusz Bromboszcz is a trade magazine publisher in Poland. The name of his principal magazine is *Medyczna Rehabilitacja*. In English, Medical Rehabilitation. In the last five years or so he has become quite successful with his publishing business. Now he is visiting the U.S. to meet with other trade publishers and to find partners for expansion plans in Europe.

Six years ago, Janusz was a Polish physician working in a hospital in Krakow. His specialty was physical therapy, and he was eking out a living for his family (a wife, two kids and some in-laws), earning about $800 per month. The family lived with even more extended family members in a grand old house that had been theirs for generations, situated on the Vistula River that runs through Krakow.

Janusz had learned to read and speak English in school, then spent some time in England, where he greatly improved his language skills. When he was still practicing medicine, he would read American medical journals, and he thought it would be wonderful if similar journals were available in Polish so that more doctors could learn from them. He envisioned starting such a magazine, but a number of roadblocks stood in his way.

Everybody in Poland was not ready for free enterprise. Decades of communist rule still affected peoples' thinking. Democracy was an idea to be debated, but not many were actually making something happen. At the time, however, there were a few Polish nationals who were already successful businessmen in other countries returning to the homeland of their fathers or grandfathers, carrying precious principles and experience. They began starting businesses, found success, and provided a great example and even greater hope to the Poles, including Janusz Bromboszcz. But he needed more details, more knowledge of the ins and outs of the magazine business.

I met Janusz as part of a contingent sponsored by the Peace Corps, which had an office in Poland designed expressly to help people like Janusz get the information they needed to follow their dreams and start businesses. I got involved about six years ago, after a wonderful, longtime employee of ours named Kay got her PhD by going to school nights. She decided to join the Peace Corps and do something worthwhile. She went off to Poland, met Janusz, understood his dream and suggested to the Peace Corps that perhaps I could help.

Poland was wonderful. I went twice.

Krakow was spared the bombing of World War II, and her museums and art were preserved. The buildings of Krakow were centuries old, and evidence of the greatness of previous generations was everywhere. Sadly, mere decades of communism had left the old city surrounded by grotesque stands of huge block buildings, apartment houses where people were taught not to think for themselves but to live for the state. When the communists fell, the buildings and much of the dependence on the state remained. These people needed new ideas. Or an old idea refit for the times.

Janusz was always way ahead of us, like a student who saw the light even before the presentation was complete. His idea moved from a vague dream to logical thoughts on paper. A business plan began to take shape. Out of this fell a financial plan, a staffing plan, a cash-flow plan and a marketing plan. It was all his, and eventually it passed any test we could apply. We planned brochures, interviewed printers, made sales calls in Warsaw in Polish and English, and trained salespeople in Polish and English.

Now Janusz Bromboszcz will travel to the U.S. as a successful businessman, seeking new ideas and partners. His potential and the potential of his business are unlimited. He will serve as a role model for many other Polish entrepreneurs.

American business can help set up this kind of success anywhere in the world. Let's do it.

○ ○ ○

Bring More to the Table Than Your Product

If you don't, you will be spouting statistics and testimonials like most other poor salespeople.

You walk into a room full of people you have never met before to have a meeting about something you are all concerned about. It could be anything from business to a homeowners meeting.

Suppose it lasts an hour or so. By the time everyone has had their say, you will have made some judgments about each other. You will have established some sort of pecking order about each of the participants in the discussion, measured your regard for them and determined a value for what each had to say.

So will everyone else in the room. Each person will make a ranking of everyone else. Who is the strongest? The weakest? Who would I like to have on my side? Who would I work for? A lot of this may not be conscious, but it still happens just below the surface.

I have been a salesman just about my whole life. I figure that my average customer has at least 25 salespeople, like me, calling on him or her. And I know that my customer has a ranking in his head for each of us. It might not be something he thinks about every day, but he could easily tell you which salespeople he hopes never call him again and which ones he is happy to hear from anytime.

So if I'm an average salesman, I'll be in the middle of the pack of that bunch of 25, and I'll probably have a hard time getting to see Mr. Big. I'll be average in my sales performance, and I'll make an average income and probably have an average life. I have probably learned to do things like most other salespeople do them.

If, on the other hand, I am not like the other 24, if I act differently, perform better, provide more information to the customer, if I really understand his problems and try to help solve them, if I sound less like I'm only interested in talking about me and my product, etc.—then things will be different for me.

I will move up in the rankings that my customer keeps in his head for his list of 25 salespeople. I will find it easier to get appointments because I will always bring value, not just my product. I will make more money than my peers, and I will probably be happier for it.

So the question for me becomes: "How can I move up in the pecking order that my customer has for all the salespeople calling on him?" I believe it comes down to a single principle. Bring a lot more to the table than your product!

How many times have you heard a sales rep (or heard yourself) say something like, "My name is Pat Wiesner and I'm with XYZ, and I'd like to stop by and drop off my card and ask you a few questions about your plans to buy our type of product to see if perhaps we might be able to help you."

What kind of ranking do you think this will get you among all the calls Mr. Big will get today? Perhaps you will be able to make a living doing that, but you will be in the middle of the pack at best.

If instead we could say something like, "I have new info about your business, how your customer buys, how your competitor sells … would you like to see it?" If we deliver on this claim we would do much better with our customer.

But to deliver on this kind of claim takes a lot of work. The top guys get it done! To be successful in any arena of business, one should be aware that everyone we deal with has a list, a pecking order.

To move up on that list we have to produce for that person. Help solve their problems first!

o o o

My Uncle and the Essence of Leadership

A few positive words can last a lifetime and shape a life.

This is most likely the first life lesson I learned. Certainly, it is the first I remember. I was around 10 years old. My family lived in Buffalo, N.Y., but I was visiting my Uncle Gil at an Army base near Washington, D.C.

It was probably 1946. The war was over, but my Uncle Gil, a colonel, was all Army, all spit and polish. He had me standing at attention, saluting (it had to be done just right) and marching while he called the cadence. I admired him a lot, and I guess for age 10, I sensed his pride and his commitment. I wanted to be just like him. And I would do anything to get his approval.

To my young eyes he was perfect in his uniform, and he took great care that everything was just right before he left the house for work each day.

One morning he brought me two pairs of shoes and asked if I knew how to shine them. Now, I had shined shoes a few times before, but I was sure that what I had done before was going to be short of what he was expecting. But I said, "Yes, sir, Uncle Gil, I'll be happy to shine them for you." So he set me up with polish and brushes and newspapers to keep me from making a mess, and put me to work.

I knew not only that these shoes were important to him, but that this was a test for me. It was incredibly important for this 10-year-old to do this right. I worked really hard. I shined every inch, particularly the tight space between the top of the shoe and the soles. When I was finished I inspected like crazy, and then I went through the whole shining process again.

Uncle Gil didn't say anything. He just sat and read his paper and didn't give me a single suggestion or correction. He gave me a job and let me do it. I am sure this was the first time anyone had done that to me. I never forgot the power of his confidence in me.

When I was satisfied that doing it again would not produce a better shine, I gave him the shoes, and I knew that whatever he said next, I would remember for a long time.

He took the shoes and turned them and looked at the heels. He turned them around again, looking at them carefully, and put them with his others. He said, "Pat, that's a wonderful job! As good as anyone! Particularly the heels; lots of people don't do as good of a job on the heels because you can't see them when the shoes are on. You'll make a good officer one day." With that he went off to do something else.

I did notice the next day that he was wearing one of the pairs of shoes that I had shined. I felt great!

As a matter of fact, I have no idea if Uncle Gil remembered that incident after I went home to Buffalo, but I have remembered it well for more than 62 years. Many times when I was doing an important or difficult job I said to myself, "Be sure to get the heels!" It sounds silly when I say it, but I'm sure that it helped me do a better job on many occasions or kept me hanging in there a little longer when it looked like all was lost.

Another important thing I learned was how powerful someone else's words, positive or negative, can be in shaping the character of another. Both will last a lifetime. Always, I've wanted to do my job as well as Uncle Gil did his. He had such a positive effect on me; I wanted to do the same for others.

If you or I want to be the best boss or the best uncle, we have a responsibility to help people see themselves in light of their strengths and relate that to who they dream of becoming.

And make sure you get the heels!

o o o

Mentoring

We don't realize the incredible effect we can have on those around us without really doing much.

Mentoring is the first job of an effective leader. If you ask people to recall teachers from their lives who were real mentors to them, they almost always come up with one or maybe two names.

We all seem to remember a couple of people who have had a big influence on our development.

And it's interesting to note that almost all the others are nameless in our memories (except the really worst).

Think now of one person who really helped you and what it has meant.

The first sort of mentor I can remember was a hockey coach from high school. He thought I could be a good hockey player and he kept telling me so. I would have tried to skate through the sideboards for that guy (and probably did so one or two times more than I should have). But I just couldn't let that man down. And it helped me to be a better player.

The first business mentor I remember was my first sales manager in Chicago. Much of how I do things to this day came from him, and most of the underlying philosophy of selling began with him. He was tough and demanding, yet he kept telling me about my strengths and how I was going to be great.

But it wasn't all just rosy reinforcement; many times he told me to "dynamite and rebuild" after a presentation or sales call. But it was always from the point of view that it was just another one of the hard-won steps on the way to becoming the salesman I really wanted to be.

Had this particular person not happened into my life I would probably never have gone into sales, or at least I never would have been successful at it.

Most of us are pretty unsure of ourselves, and we get so little feedback on the subject that we listen intently when we get some from a source that is important to us.

You and I are potentially that important source for all those who work for us and all those we work with.

What could be more fulfilling and enjoyable than helping someone achieve his or her own success? We simply need to decide that we are going to be a power for the achievements of others.

And fortunately, there is a formula!

This formula was given to me years ago by a man named Bob James, a motivational trainer (and another early mentor of mine). Like many formulae for human relations, this one is easy to say but takes a lot of effort to put into practice. If you have four or five people around you, employees or coworkers that you care about, you can be a huge influence in their lives with this. And it is particularly powerful when motivating children. Here it is: Help someone see himself or herself in light of a personal strength they are unaware of or are unsure of.

Ideally it will be related to the person they dream of becoming. Look for genuine strengths that will help them be what they want to become.

Doing this in your family will make you the best parent, brother, mother, husband possible.

Doing this in your company will make you invaluable. The very hardest people to find in business are those few who enjoy and cause the success of others.

Becoming Top Management

Meaning the best, not the most senior. A company is fortunate
when both concepts come together.

The goal of most aspiring managers is to reach top management. All middle managers probably will tell you they hope to either work their way into top management or own their own company.

My experience is that the top people at any level in a good company invariably move up to the next level. The way to move up is to be tops at your present management job. Sometimes, however, people don't understand how to be a top manager.

For example, we had a sales manager who knocked the cover off the ball on his magazine, but couldn't understand why management wouldn't reward him by making him publisher. The basic reason was he used the people around him, the ones helping him achieve his sales goals, as stepping stones. He didn't care much about them or their careers.

He didn't realize this characteristic was a requirement for the next job up the line. He wasn't yet top management material.

Some food for thought as we all work out our own way of becoming top management:

Top management is always replenishing and replacing itself. Want to know who senior management considers the best managers in your company, the ones who will zoom up the ladder? Look for those openly bringing along new management candidates. They constantly look for, and promote, new people.

A good question for you or those you manage is, "Who have you got coming along to take your place?"

A manager who doesn't develop and train good, new managers probably never will make it to one of the corner offices.

Top management should not be like a private and exclusive club. Senior management might be so at some companies, but top managers never think the only important people are at their level or higher. Many act as if that is what they believe.

To be tops, talk to, and particularly listen to, people at all levels. Not only will you learn a lot about how your company works, but you also will develop a positive reputation. It will help you find people you will want to inspire to move up in management.

If you're in senior management, make yourself accessible, attentive and responsive. Time spent just wandering around your company, talking and listening to people at all levels, will be some of the best top management time you can spend. People will feel part of a team only if they feel included. One of the most important jobs of senior management is to make everyone in the company know they are included.

Top management knows and understands all of its people. Know the people around you, above you, below you and at the same level. Know them well enough to know if they have ambitions inside the company, outside the company or, perhaps, if they have "retired" but not left the company.

Know who contributes and who doesn't. Grow the contributors. Try to help the noncontributors. But in the end, the noncontributors must be removed for the sake of the contributors.

Getting to the next level of management is more than a reward for a job well done at the present level. It means being entrusted with a larger piece of the company's future and the hopes and aspirations of all its people. Only top managers should move up.

Those Flocking Boids

I watched a flock of birds or a school of fish and wondered just what mystical management principles were at work to keep the formation intact.

While not a big-time scuba diver, I really like it. The magnificent colors, the sense of mystery and the abundant and somewhat strange life forms are endlessly fascinating. Even when you're with other swimmers, the experience is heightened by the feeling of being alone—a feeling that I attribute to the dependency on your breathing apparatus. To float along a Caribbean reef at 50 or 60 feet and carefully inspect the plants and little animals that flourish there never seems to get tiresome. Particularly awesome are the huge schools of tiny, brilliantly colored or luminescent fish, literally millions in a group and acting as one. When one turns, they all tum. It's the same with a stampeding herd or flock of starlings. They seem to start, stop and dart as a unit.

Now how do they do that? These little fish whose brains can't be the size of a grain of rice, swimming in formation with a few hundred thousand brethren and never missing a beat, never seeming to be out of step. How does God do that? How do they communicate? How do they all know what every other one is going to do, and then all do it together with such precision?

It's one of nature's most beautiful and wondrous sights—one you usually only get to see if you're willing to go scuba diving. It's something that I have marveled at and been mystified by for years. I still marvel, but at least some of the mystery is gone since I came across "Boids" in a book I have been trying to read titled *Complexity*.

Boids is a computer simulation invented by Craig Reynolds of the Los Angeles Symbolics Corp. It accurately captures the essence of flocking birds, herding sheep or schooling fish. Simply put, it's a screen full of Boids (bird-like entities) along with moving objects, where they obey only three rules:

1. Attempt to maintain a minimum distance from all other Boids and objects on the screen.
2. Attempt to match speed with other Boids in the neighborhood.
3. Attempt to move to the center of the Boids in the neighborhood.

The result: perfect schooling of the fish (Boids)! The little computer creatures stay in formation, while flowing around the moving objects and walls just like a real-life school, flock or herd.

What is fascinating is the simplicity of it all. No telepathy, no mystic link to one "guru" Boid and no huge system or network: only simple rules applied locally.

We often make life too complicated and mysterious—including business and management. Might there be a way to apply this kind of thinking to management?

Well, the whole reason for this column is that I recently ran into two other businessmen who had read the same book, *Complexity*. We talked about Boids and tried to come up with a list of locally applicable, simple rules that would get good results in management if earnestly applied. Here are our candidates:

1. Attempt to give a lot of credit to the people around you.
2. Attempt to convince the people who work for you that you truly care about their future.
3. Attempt to give your organization clear goals and achievable objectives.

The objective of good management is to get the "best work" out of people and cause them to take pride in working as a team to achieve at a level that makes them proud, confident and assured of a better future for themselves and the team.

Everyone knows the value of "credit." People who get lots of credit, give lots of credit.

Employees will identify with a boss or manager who they are sure will help them achieve his or her goals in the process of achieving their own goals.

An atmosphere of openness where everyone on the team knows the objective is necessary if a real sense of team and team accomplishment is to be realized.

It would seem that the application of some simple, natural rules will help us all be better managers and take advantage of the natural tendency of people to want to be in an environment where they can be in formation and in unison with others.

o o o

Another Kind of American Export

Our way of business is respected and envied the world over: this
report from the Panama Canal.

You think you know your wife of many years until she says one day,
"You know, I've always wanted to go through the Panama Canal."
Well, since the canal was soon to be turned back to the Panamanians, we
decided to do it sooner rather than later. We got there a couple of weeks
before the turnover.

Two things impressed us greatly. The first was the realization of the
incredible engineering feat that is the Panama Canal. It is about 50 miles
long. In the late 1800s, the Frenchman who had built the Suez Canal,
Ferdinand de Lesseps, had hoped to become an even greater hero of the
times by connecting the Atlantic with the Pacific through what was then
Colombia. He tried for years to build a trench connecting the oceans.
After some 20,000 workers died from dysentery, malaria, yellow fever and
snakebite, they gave up, defeated and bankrupt.

Enter Teddy Roosevelt and an engineer named John Stevens. New
drugs helped deal with the bugs, and a new concept for removing the dirt
got them started. The key was to abandon the idea of a ditch in favor of a
system of locks. They created a lake in the middle of the isthmus from the
rain-forest runoff, which provides a head of water to operate a set of three
locks on each end of the canal.

You sail into the first lock (able to hold huge ships). The rear gates
are closed and valves are opened in pipes the size of the Holland Tunnel,
channeling water from the lake above into the lock. In less than 15 minutes
you and your boat have risen 30 feet and are being towed into the next lock.
And so, on up to the lake, across and then down on the other side in a like
fashion to the other ocean in less than six hours.

Certainly, this is one of the top engineering feats of the millennium
and the first major export of American know-how and technology.

The second and more important impression was gained from a number
of Panamanians and best stated by a young lady in the Panama airport. I

asked her how she felt about the U.S. leaving.

She said, "It's good for my country but there is one big disadvantage. When you go to work for an American company, or the military, it doesn't matter where you were born or what your family name is. If you work hard you can advance. This is not usually true in Panama."

This is the bedrock of America's strength domestically and internationally. It is what is missing in so many other places and the reason so many want to come here.

Three Simple Ways to Be a Better Manager

To tap the strength of your workers, get to know them.

It is the time of year to be resolving to do things a little better. I recently came across these ideas that will make us all better managers and people. Here are three simple ideas:

- Get out of your office.
- Ask two extra questions.
- Convince people they "can do it."

I think they will pay huge dividends.

Get out of your office. Just walk around, talk to people, zone, be interested, be a human being. Talk to people about everything—business, the ball game, everything.

Some managers don't realize just how intimidating the boss's office is. Particularly if he happens to be one of those who build sort of a citadel of their office, with a conference table for staff with his/her desk at the head. When we have been summoned to the boss's office we are on guard, on our best behavior, and we have all our defensive filters operating.

If you and I are really interested in finding out what makes people tick, if we really want to communicate with the people on our team, we will do much better sitting in their office than in ours.

Don't bring problems from your office to theirs; bring interest in them with you at the top of the menu.

Ask two extra questions.

One of your kids comes in asking, "Can I go to the midnight movie with my friends?" or one of your team says, "I have a plan that's better than yours," or your customer says, "Sorry, but we think your competitor has better quality."

We are all pretty much spring-loaded to respond to these types of situations defensively and negatively. In doing so we serve clear notice whether we want to or not that we are not interested in new ideas, an open mind or in trusting our kids.

Skillful managers and leaders will stop and ask a couple of questions that give the other person a chance to explain and sell their idea. It gives you a chance to get more information to make your decisions. And it sends a signal that we are willing to listen. That automatically makes us a better boss, parent or sales rep than 90 percent who are out there.

Convince people they "can do it."

We were wandering around a shop in downtown Littleton before a play at the Littleton Town Hall Arts Center (really a neat place) where I saw a cup with a thoughtful saying printed on it. It seems that this is mostly what cups are good for these days. It said, "If you could not fail, what would you try to do?" It made me think of the best bosses I have had, and they both were really good at making me feel like "I could do it!" I knew what they expected of me, and I knew that they sincerely wanted me to be successful. So I did everything in my power to achieve their goals. My own goals came along for the ride.

Let's tell people in our lives (everyone—kids, friends and employees) about their strengths, give them a reputation to live up to, give them something to achieve ... and then stand back.

So:
• Get out of your office and meet the real people.
• Ask a couple extra questions and learn more.
• Convince people that "they can do it" and they will!

Have a good year!

o o o

Growth by Association

We may or may not be "what we eat," but we are probably going to end up being like the people we like working for.

It was one of the most important sales calls of the year. It took place in Chicago at the offices of one of the most prestigious advertising agencies in existence. There was to be a room full of account executives and media buyers, and the two presenters were early so that they could set up their presentation of flip charts and slides.

The presentation was for a lot of marbles because the agency had the most accounts of any agency in the territory that could buy advertising from these salesmen.

The junior of the two was really nervous because this was his first really big show. He busied himself setting up equipment, thinking it would make him feel more comfortable.

At the appointed hour, the room filled up with important people. The senior salesman greeted each and made some small talk while the junior one quietly checked his notes just one more time, hoping against hope that his small part would go well and all questions would be directed to his mentor.

About a dozen people sat around the conference table and the carefully set-up electronic equipment. The room quieted and the senior salesman began to speak. The young salesman knew it would be his time to talk in about five minutes, and he wondered if he would have a heart attack first, his heart was beating so fast. The certainty of an attack became clear immediately. The newer salesman's boss was saying something the younger man had never heard before and didn't expect.

"We have come here today to tell you about our magazine, and all the reasons that you should buy full advertising schedules for all your accounts with us," the older man said.

"This presentation is planned to last just 30 minutes. But I know that you have been giving thought to these decisions and that you have been using our magazine this past year. So, if you have already decided to advertise with us as much or more, we can skip this half-hour presentation and go right to a celebratory lunch!"

The young salesman (who happened to be me!) was stunned. During the next few seconds of silence, I thought all was lost.

Finally, the agency president said, "John, let's go to lunch; we love your magazine!"

And that was that.

This happened at least 35 years ago. But on that day I learned volumes about "closing"—so much so that I remember the meeting today in all its detail. I learned that the art of closing was merely getting an answer to the question, "What work is there to be done here before they will buy?"

I decided I could learn a lot from John, and to stick to him like glue. And learn I did.

Now, to this day, I try to pass on the lessons I learned from my early sales mentor.

How can we become successful? There are many aspects to the answer, but one thing that you almost always find in people on their way up is that they find mentors—people they admire, and with whom they develop a relationship based on learning. My advice: find people that you admire, tell them your goals, ask their advice and try it! If you can't find anyone like that at your company, leave and find work where you can.

And if you are in charge, make sure that you and the rest of your managers are people worth following.

o o o

Getting the Job

There is more to it than just being competent.

I recently overheard a professional placement service representative giving advice to a highly qualified job applicant seeking employment with a major airline.

"When you go in for your interview, wear a dark blue suit, white shirt, conservative tie, black shoes with laces and have a three-day-old haircut," the advisor says.

The young man challenges the advisor, "What if I wear my dress loafers with the nice tassels: Will that keep me from getting a job as a pilot?" The advisor says, "I don't know for sure, but I do know that these things count and are noted in writing in your interview file. The airlines wouldn't even talk to you unless you were an outstanding pilot. Now they want to see what kind of person you are in addition to that."

What a tough thing it is to interview for a new job today, whether in your own company or another. Some interviewers purposely play mind games to uncover the real you. Others conduct an interview to test if you can remember all the facts from your résumé.

Outside of the competence issue, there are two things that move me in prospective employee interviews:

Be interested and enthusiastic. Yesterday was primary day here in Colorado. I voted at about 6 p.m. in a precinct where there are some 1,500 registered Republicans. When I asked how many of us had voted, a woman said, rather embarrassed as though it was her fault, that only 87 people had done so.

Then last night I went to the Avalanche hockey game with two high-school seniors who talked for 10 minutes about how excited they were to finally be 18 this year so they could vote. They each had opinions and preferences as to how they would use their vote.

I would rather hire either young man, with his positive view of the world and his place in it, than anyone of the 1,413 Republican adults who skipped the primary because their vote didn't count, or the system is rigged, or the candidates weren't worth it or whatever.

So often when older people lose jobs or are replaced by younger workers, they blame management greed, saying something like, "I have all the experience and knowledge, I can do this job in my sleep, yet they chose to replace me with this kid. It's only because they can get him/her cheaper! Greedy bastards!"

I suppose at times this is true, but I think what management is really "greedy" for is positive people. People who see a bright future for themselves and their company. People who say, "Give the problem to me, I can solve it for us." People who want to be involved and counted, in business and in elections.

A good interviewer is trying, along with other things, to place you on this important scale. Help him/her. Be open, be honest, be yourself and be interested.

You should be excited by the prospect of this new job or you wouldn't be there. However, give the interviewer the same credit you would expect for yourself. He/she easily will spot a phony who's spreading it too thick.

Be curious. This goes deeper than just asking questions. Forget about getting the job for a while and concentrate on learning about this company, this job and this person. You want answers to these questions:

What kind of people work there? How does management treat people? Is it a pleasant place to work?

(Listen while you are in the reception area; eavesdrop in the hallways. Are these folks happy?)

What are this company's goals? Will you fit in?

How did this person become successful with this company?

You are there to be interviewed, so listen and answer. But ask a lot of your own questions. It serves two purposes. First, you will get the information. Second, it will reveal your curiosity, personality and interests to the interviewer.

That's half the purpose of the meeting anyway.

o o o

The Power of Approval and Participation

People always try to describe the difference between leadership and management. Some managers also are leaders, some aren't. Here's what I have learned.

You know how it is after a long, hard day of skiing. My wife was looking for a new ski jacket and moved from store to store, looking at jacket after jacket. Occasionally, she would try one on and ask my opinion.

I was beat, shuffling behind, carrying the other package and the old jacket. I always muttered approval when my opinion was sought ("That really looks good on you; let's get that one!") in an attempt to advance the post-ski progression: home, snack, shower and nap.

This day was a little different, however. We had a guest, a friend from back East, a man I considered normal, more or less. Therefore, I expected he would shuffle along with me, commiserate in the ancient manner and make the best of it.

But it was not to be. I was shocked into speechlessness when my friend—let's call him Alan—handed me his jacket in the manner one would hang an unwanted slicker on a horse, quickly joined my wife and said, "Janet, I love to shop! And I'm good at it. Let's find something perfect for you."

She didn't miss a beat. Together, they dove into a forest of polyester and down. In no time, after much flourish and comparison, they joyfully made a coat selection and also picked some accessories that made everyone happy.

Notwithstanding the near sinful betrayal of his gender, Alan made me think about the power of approval and participation. In this little vignette, his attitude and involvement made two and two equal five. Because of his leadership, much was accomplished and everybody was happy.

Who is more a leader, the Marine who leads men up the hill to take the pillbox or the one who commands his unit up the hill?

The sales manager who makes calls with his/her salesmen/saleswomen is a better leader than one who merely manages the calls.

The best manager (leader) I ever met was like that. Every day, you'd get the message that he liked what you were doing and wanted to help. He wanted to participate—not in a way that replaced you ("Give me that hammer; I can hit the nail much better than you can") but in a supportive manner to help you achieve your goals.

Even when he didn't like what I was doing, I knew he valued me and my contribution. When we disagreed, it was in an atmosphere of approval and participation. He made it clear if I looked good, he was happy for the positive reflection on him as a manager (leader).

What ingredients must be added to a manager to make a leader? It is probably a good book topic. But here are two key ingredients:

A leader creates an atmosphere of approval and acceptance in which the group can operate.

A leader participates in a supportive way and takes great pleasure in the success of individuals in the group. And everyone knows it.

Sales Manager

It's a truly tough job to fill. When do you know you have a good one?

Why is sales manager the toughest job in the company? Because you can't possibly understand the job unless you have been an "in the trenches" salesperson yourself, yet selling does very little to prepare one for the job. Most often the best salesperson in the company is promoted to sales manager, leaving two holes in the sales effort: one in the territory just vacated, the other in the position of sales manager. Despite the obvious weaknesses of this system, we in business are likely to continue to use it because when you can connect sales success to the following traits and characteristics, you get a real winner.

Mentor: A salesman takes pleasure in his or her own performance and struts every success. This is how he or she refuels. The sales manager takes pleasure in seeing others being successful. For those salespeople who become good sales managers, there seems to be a point where they put aside their "center-stage" needs in favor of "coaching." They reach a point where they get their "limelight" by watching their charges perform. The salespeople who work for a really effective sales manager know without reservation that their boss truly wants them to have the best future possible.

Listener: Good salespeople are supposed to be good listeners, but sales managers must be better. They must understand the product, the customer, the salesperson, the market, the results, the problems, etc. The good ones seem always to be asking questions and listening to answers only to ask another question.

Motivator: During tough times, the outstanding sales manager understands the pain and helps the salesperson survive and learn. In good times he or she uses the success to help the salesperson achieve to new levels. What comes through to the managed is the genuine concern of the manager. The test: Are your salespeople thinking, "With my boss's support, I will sell more and achieve more than I ever thought possible!"?

Drill Sergeant: Salespeople hate paperwork and reports. Sales managers love them. A good sales manager will get his or her crew to at least accept this stuff as a tool to help everyone do a better job. This requires a tough-minded person who expects and gets paperwork execution. No department is well run that does not document expectations and performance.

Teacher: The sales manager must help his or her people learn to be better, and he or she has to pass along lessons learned along the way. But this has to be done with skill and encouragement. So often it is not. Everyone in sales has a war story or two about making calls with a sales manager that used the occasion to illustrate just how smart he or she was and how dumb the salesperson was. Unfortunately, this sort of person usually likes to play to an audience so that the humiliation is public! Managers who feed on the denigration of those managed, in any department, should be sent to the competition! At the very least, send them packing!

Team Builder: When you notice that your salespeople take pleasure in the successes of other salespeople, take a long admiring look at your sales manager. There is team building going on here. Your success is mine, and vice versa. This can only take place in a positive, reinforcing, you-can't-really-make-a-bad-mistake atmosphere.

It's the responsibility of the department manager. Of course, if the opposite is true, it is still the responsibility of the department manager.

Example: At the core of good selling is honesty and integrity. A company's image begins with a sales manager's example, leveraged out into the community by the sales force's behavior.

Is it any wonder that sales manager is such a good training ground for top management?

o o o

"Herb, Could You Come to My Office Please?"

There are better ways to command than from behind a desk.

Several weeks ago, there was a story on TV about the reopening of the Statue of Liberty to visitors following the Sept. 11, 2001, attacks on New York. The piece sort of revolved around the Park Service manager responsible for the place. He talked of how he saw his job as being in charge of the quality of the experience offered to "his" visitors.

After Liberty Island begins to fill up with a couple boatloads of people, the manager's technique is to roam everywhere, mixing, talking, asking and answering questions and generally trying to discover what people wanted from their visit, and then seeing to it that they get it. He calls it "Management by Walking."

It looked like most people got back on the boat happy.

After seeing the story, I couldn't help thinking about some managers I've seen who look at management in a totally different way.

Some treat management as something to be administered smartly from the corner office.

When an instruction needs to be given, or a correction needs to be made, or praise needs to be handed out, everybody is summoned to the big guy's office so that protocol is observed, and so that everyone is totally aware that whatever the decision is about, it came down from above.

I worked for a guy once who had an office three times as big as any other in the company, and his desk stood on an eight-inch platform. All meetings with him were conducted in that office. Everyone knew he was sending a message by making his office a stage on which he would communicate anything that was important to him, and yet he had no problem leaving that office when a potential business deal called for it.

The biggest office, the nicest chair, the seat at the head of the table and the last word are all things that most people expect the boss to take, and actually some people might even prefer it that way. But a really good boss also knows that it takes a lot more to get respect, cooperation and the very best work from people.

People who manage only from a position of power miss the boat.

They need to do like the manager of the Liberty Island Park Service and get out of the office, walk, talk, learn and communicate.

Great managers know their people well. Not so much as "buddies" but as people with goals and business ambitions. So:

Come out of the corner office sometimes: stroll, talk, ask, answer.

Get to know every member of your team in terms of their goals and dreams. If you help someone achieve his or her goals, that person will help you reach yours.

Extend the definition of your office. Make your "office" everywhere you do business, everywhere in your building, everywhere you have team members.

Don't always summon. Go and see.

Occasionally, sit for a few minutes and get to know someone at your plant who you don't normally talk to.

Our challenge as leaders and managers is to bring out the best in people. Leaders who get around often get a lot more done.

Define Yourself

There's nothing like having a good picture of where you're going to help you get there.

About 30 years ago I rented a room in Palo Alto, Calif., for a couple of months from a wonderful lady named Paige. I had gone to California to pursue a new career track in my younger days, leaving behind my wife and young family for a few weeks while I got started in a new job in a new place.

Paige was a widow about 60 years old who had a couple of rooms that she rented to itinerants like me. When I wasn't working, I hung around the house watching TV and often spent time talking to Paige, an interesting and gracious lady.

I noticed that she had a number of little statues of elegant ballerinas around the house, and one day I asked her what was up with these figurines.

"Well," she said, "they are my model, my inspiration. I have a problem with my weight, and those little gals remind me from all over my house what my goal is." She then proceeded to tell me just how effective they had been and how much weight she had lost. She finished by telling me that a young man such as myself should have goals in order to succeed.

When I first met Warren he was a new salesman. Probably in his third sentence he told me he wanted to be a publisher (in our business that's like being manager of a business unit). He went on to say he knew that his chance would depend on his ability to sell advertising space, and he decided that he was going to be one of the best. He also said that he would spend all his office time talking to people who could buy and that he would never do paperwork during the day, only at night, when he couldn't talk to potential buyers.

Warren not only told me but he told everyone what his goal was and how he was going to get there. He defined himself for himself and for everyone who knew him. I'm sure I don't need to tell you that he reached every one of his goals and went far beyond them. Over time his goals changed, but he always knew what they were.

One of my kids played soccer in high school for a coach who told me that his No. 1 job was to make the boys feel good about themselves and the game. He defined himself as a builder of young men. He never shouted or screamed (as a matter of fact, he didn't let parents do it, either). He was fair but demanding and he loved to win.

But he loved building young men even more. He was successful because his goals were clear and he knew what he had to do to be successful. He developed some really good soccer players and some even better young men.

If you and I want to be more successful than we are, we should think about the person we want to be, then define ourselves in terms of a vision of this successful person. In effect, we will fill our "house" with statuettes of our model for ourselves that will remind us of what we want to be and where we should channel our energy and our actions.

O O O

On Your Own

So, you're thinking of starting a business? The dream seems to make more sense when times are tough.

The biggest job of top management in our company is to create an atmosphere where top people will want to spend their careers. A lot of people are content to work for the right company, I'm happy to say, but for some, the appeal and attraction of "my own business" is irresistible.

For some, like me, it was a near necessity.

People are always curious and interested in how this company got started. Even more so now that there are more good managers either out of work or considering the prospect of starting their own businesses. This company, Wiesner Publishing, was started in a recession (at least a tough downturn).

I was working for a small publishing company here in Colorado as president and I had a disagreement with the owner. I quit and he fired me almost in the same breath. Who was actually first is lost in the thickening fog of time. Anyway, I was out of work at the beginning of an economic downturn. So, 20 years ago, in 1982, we started this outfit on a shoestring with an idea and lots of energy. I have always enjoyed working for good companies, particularly in the publishing business ... it's a kick. But there is nothing like having your own business.

So, what's my advice to someone thinking of going off on their own?

PASSION. It doesn't matter if you are going into business with an idea that you have thought about for years or whether you are going to buy into a business already in place. You must feel so strongly about your new venture that you will be willing to do almost anything and even to lose everything to make it work. This passion will not only help you the many times that the going gets tough, it will also be signaled to your clients, suppliers, family and workers. It will be a critical source of strength for everyone.

PLAN. You must have a well-thought-out plan. Good enough to make you think that you can get rich. Good enough for you to make a lot of sacrifices along the way. Test your plan on friends, potential customers and industry experts. Make sure it has no holes.

MONEY. It doesn't always take a great deal of money, but you have to get it somewhere. Basically, there are five sources: (1) banks, (2) venture capitalists, (3) public money or the stock market, (4) an angel investor (your rich Aunt Emma who wants to fund your every idea), and (5) yourself.

1. Banks will lend you money if you have collateral to protect their money. Start-up businesses usually don't have collateral, except equities the founder might have (like his or her home).
2. VCs require a huge upside, a great plan, and they will want an agreement that makes you go bankrupt if the idea fails. This is how they guarantee your "passion." Big ideas (Intel, FedEx, etc.) get started this way.
3. Public money can be available. Expensive: You will have lots of financial partners.
4. If you can use money from Aunt Emma, do it!
5. This leaves you, which is the way many begin. Starting from scratch, you need enough money to get you beyond the initial investment stages. Don't fool yourself about this. The most common reason small businesses fail is that they are undercapitalized.

PEOPLE. You will need the skills and people power to implement your plan. Not only will they need money, they will need to be managed and led. People work for salary. They also work for a sense of accomplishment and inclusion. If you're good with people, going into business will be easier; if you're not, get a partner who is.

CASH. Remember: The most important word in business is cash. When you are out of cash, you are out of business. Plan to never run out!

o o o

Right Rudder!

A manager's words always matter.

A long time ago I decided that I wanted to learn how to fly. What really happened was my wife gave me one of those $15 trial flights for my birthday, and I've been at it ever since. But a couple of times, early instructors almost made me quit. I particularly remember one guy who seemed to try very hard to make something that I enjoyed into something that I dreaded.

Intimidators are lousy managers. When first learning to do a takeoff in a single-engine aircraft, the fledging pilot must learn to apply right rudder to compensate for the left turning tendency due to engine torque. In the beginning it's not the most instinctive thing to do, so beginners need to be reminded from time to time. What my nemesis would do is remind me by shouting louder each time, "Right rudder! RIGHT RUDDER, RIGHT RUDDER!" He would then add remarks about how even the dumbest recruit could tell his right foot from the left and how one has to have an IQ higher than 50 to be a pilot. It got so that I couldn't have found my right foot with both hands.

Session after session, all I tried to do was please the man rather than to understand or learn what it was I needed to learn. I don't remember how I outlasted that guy, but the time it took me to learn to fly was longer because of him. I almost decided not to learn at all (because I thought it was too tough for me).

What we say to people and how we say it can have a big effect on what they learn and, more importantly, how they feel about themselves and you. Avoid at all costs working for or being any of the following:

Ego Dracula. There are some people who seem to feel better about themselves only if they can diminish someone else. A couple of years ago I went to a business meeting where the boss thought he was entertaining us and proving to us just how smart he was by constantly belittling his second in command. He would say something about how nearly incompetent his lieutenant was and then look at us out of the corner of his eye as if to get approval. I didn't have the courage to say anything then, but I have often thought of that No. 2 man, wondering if he ever escaped to a job where he could feel good about himself and even grow.

Bully. The best example of these are "screamers." Anyone who raises their voice to a co-worker or subordinate should be fired on the spot. If they are allowed to get away with it, they can do a lot of damage to your department or your company. Mostly they will run off anyone with real potential.

Just plain better. These people simply make it clear that the rest of us are inferior. They usually use position to do it. No one else can have an idea, no one else can really be trusted, every decision must be approved and every action agreed to ahead of time. Anyone who works for someone like this will hate their job.

Each of these types can be spotted around the Little League fields. If you want to really find out what kind of manager a person will be, watch them around their children. They identify themselves by saying things like "Give me that hammer, you'll never learn to pound a nail!" or "That was really stupid when you passed the ball to Tommy!" or "Shut up!" They often make it 10 times worse by doing these things in front of others. These people are bad parents and will surely be rotten managers.

Good managers, good parents and good people have the insight to give honest, helpful feedback that helps people improve and grow while at the same time ensuring a growing self-image and self-confidence. If self-image and self-confidence aren't growing, competence, insight and ability are not growing, either.

o o o

Success Comes in Cans

There can be no success without doing something hard. Our ticket to the top is something distasteful and difficult we would rather delay. Such a simple concept. But it seems hard for us to keep in mind, all of the time for some of us and some of the time for all of us.

A friend relayed a recent conversation he had with his college freshman son. It went something like this:

"Dad, I want to drop physics."

"OK. How come?"

"Well, tomorrow is the last day I can drop it and just take an incomplete. If I drop it before the deadline, it won't hurt my grades. I can take it again later when things are a little more settled and I can get a better grade."

"Yeah. But what makes you want to drop it in the first place?"

"Well, first, the teacher stinks. He makes it really hard to learn. I really don't like it; it's hard and I can't do it properly at this time. I know I'll need it eventually to get into med school but I'd really like to do it later when it'll be easier. OK, Dad? This will save my GPA for this semester, and I promise I'll do better later when I take physics again. Sound like a plan?"

"Well, son ... "

Sound familiar? Maybe you have been on one side or the other of this talk. We all have. See if what that father told his son makes sense.

" ... Dropping physics probably won't make much difference for your career in the long run. If you think that it's best, let's do it. As you know, we still have to pay for the hours, but you do what you think is best.

"I know that this is going to sound like a lecture and I apologize up front. But let me tell you something I have learned many times in my life. I learned it in college, I learned it again in my first job and yet another time when I first became a manager. And that is that nothing really good happens until you do something hard. The opportunity to excel, to do great work, to jump a few steps on the ladder always comes in the form of something hard, something I hate doing and would rather put off.

"You can drop physics, but that only means that you will have to wait for the next 'opportunity,' something that needs to be done that I guarantee will be hard, you won't like and would rather put off.

"Without some opportunity, something really hard to do, there can be no real success! You must decide when. But only after sticking with and accomplishing something you really would rather have not messed with, will you feel the true meaning of success, self-confidence and accomplishment. And when the next 'opportunity' comes along, it will be somewhat easier to deal with."

Successful people at every stage of life keep encountering tough projects. Whenever we start taking the easier road and leaving the hard stuff to others, we become less successful.

My old friend and mentor from Dale Carnegie, LuVaine G. (Boo) Bue, used to give an inspirational speech called "Success Comes in Cans." He knew failure comes in Cant's. For all of us.

Why Chuck Couldn't Make It to the Top

The mistake of seeing success as a hill to climb alone

Chuck was a terrific salesman. From his first day at being what he playfully called "a peddler," it was clear that he had a real gift for it. Everything he worked on seemed to result in a sale. Every one of his customers and teammates enjoyed his easygoing manner and fun-loving and sometimes seemingly careless way of dealing with problems.

He worked hard. He started early every day and prided himself on being able to make more calls in a week than any other salesperson in the business. He learned everything there was to know about his product. He studied the competition until he could give their presentation as well as his own.

He worked smart. He knew that "selling time" (the time spent talking to someone who can buy your product) was his most precious commodity. So, he would either meet prospects face-to-face or talk to them on the phone during the work day and take planning and paperwork home at night.

He enjoyed and deserved the spotlight at national sales meetings. The attention he earned was part of his motivation. He was always doing something creative. One time he gave a power-point presentation on the wall next to his table at a restaurant to the delight of the other patrons and the amusement of his client, who ended up buying a lot.

In short, he loved his job and the popularity that came with it. He was a great salesman and he shot right to the top. He made more money, had more friends in and out of the company and was the No.1 prospect for advancement. He had earned the right to try management, where he could try to bring others to the same success he had achieved. And he soon got his chance.

Less than a year later, though, he was history. Gone.

He had failed as a manager. No one who worked for him benefited from his leadership, and the entire team was just so-so.

He had to be removed as a leader, and he wouldn't take a sales job again, so he left.

What happened? How is it that someone with so much potential could end up out of the system altogether?

Basically, he could never give up the spotlight. He wanted to use his sales team to promote himself, as a ladder to climb, rather than to motivate the team to excel so its members could achieve what they wanted to accomplish.

He never came to realize that the quickest way to the top is to make other people successful. He didn't get it that the most valuable kind of manager is the one in a hundred who enjoys engineering the success of others. He never realized that management at most companies looks long and hard for people who can grow other people.

Most managers can't get to the top unless they take one or more people with them. The more people they help to succeed, the higher they go.

So how do you know if you can be good at that?

Here's a little self-test:

- Do you enjoy the success of others as much as your own?
- Do you like to help your peers solve their problems?
- Is your image of a leader one who gets the best work out of others?
- Do you take time with others to find out what they would like to accomplish, then help them develop the ability, knowledge and confidence to accomplish it?

True leaders are hard to find. But this is what makes them tick.

o o o

Keeping Your Word

If an employee has done a good job for a long time—to the point you almost have forgotten them—perhaps it's time to ask, "How am I doing?"

We recently lost a very good employee. She was topnotch in just about every way, especially her attitude. She never said "no," not even "maybe." She just did what she was asked, efficiently and thoroughly.

She was cheerful, pleasant and eager. She regularly threw her hat into the ring when a better position opened up and later earned a promotion.

She learned very quickly, helped others easily and was just the kind of employee you would like to have. I'm sure she would have been successful in our company.

But she gave two weeks' notice.

She had been looking for a couple of months and went with another publishing company. She had approached them, not the other way around. By the time we found out, it was too late to do anything. She had inquired, negotiated and accepted before we knew we had a problem. Her mind was made up and there was nothing we could do.

What happened? How can we learn from this? How can we keep it from happening again?

What we learned made us question our managerial skills.

About a year earlier, along with the excitement and intensity that comes with a minor restructuring, we had promised her she would learn a new side of business in her new job. We promised she would learn the production side, how to physically make magazines. We promised courses, seminars and involvement in an interesting part of the business, and this excited her about the new job.

Well, we never really delivered. After an initial flurry, everybody went back to putting out fires and we, at least for a time, forgot about our commitment. And, as they say, the rest is history.

How do we prevent this from happening again?

Talk to your employees. The most embarrassing thing is that this was such a surprise to everyone on our management team. And our company is small enough that any one of us should have known what was happening—though this could happen in any size company.

You don't have to read this column more than once a year to know I'm always talking about knowing the importance of knowing the goals and aspirations of your employees.

Well, this is a good example of what happens when you don't. One of us should have been asking her, "How's it going? Do you like your job? Is it what you thought it would be?"

Don't be smug. When things are going well and you're feeling complacent, that is the time to ask yourself, "How am I doing?" Ask this question about everybody you care about. Tell them if you don't ask them often enough, they should tell you anyway.

Keep your promises. Care to guess what percentage of management's promises are kept? Well, let's decide you and I are going to do better than average. Write them down and revisit them regularly.

If we do whatever it takes to be the kind of company that delivers what it promises to employees, we will attract the best people in our industry.

2001: The Year of Value

What makes a stock worthwhile is the same thing that makes anything worthwhile.

In an effort to be able to write about what people may be thinking about the stock market, I routinely have meetings with professionals who should know.

Last week I spent an interesting 90 minutes with some prominent trust-fund managers. As you can imagine, all they had to be proud of were those instances where a fund beat some market average, all of which were down. For example, a fund down 3 percent for the year would have been up 8 percent over the S&P 500, which was down 11 percent on the year.

Anecdotes about whipsawing dotcom fortunes are plentiful. Young entrepreneurs and investors found themselves worth a million or two and were convinced that the new economy was going to deliver 25 percent per year for the anointed. "A couple of years of this and I can retire young," they figured. Suddenly though, in one year they have lost half their dream; more in some cases.

What's next? Just about everyone says "back to basics." Stock prices will reflect stock value. A stock will have real value directly proportional to its ability to earn a return for its owner. All those companies with the strange names that you can't spell are going to have to have a PIE greater than zero. By the way, our trust-fund friends told us that they expect 2001 will bring the market up about 10 percent. We'll see.

In the meantime, it will serve us well to think about value. As we prepare for a new year, let's ask ourselves about the value in our relationships, in our jobs and in all the important parts of life.

Value in management. Where should a manager invest to create value? Clearly in his people. It seems so simple, but many managers don't get it. A manager cannot grow unless his or her people grow. It seems to me that in our company, the No. 1 reason that some sales managers peak in that position is because they never really get out of their own way and facilitate and rejoice in the success of their people. The year 2001 is a good time to renew our commitment to build people. Not only will it be rewarding to us, but it is exactly what our own management will be looking for.

Value in sales. How does a salesperson invest to create value for his/her future? By putting his/her customer first, before even commissions and sales. Two seemingly contradictory personalities must come together in the successful salesperson. First is the person who hates to lose, a vicious competitor who is willing to invest nearly all his/her time and effort to win. Second is the person who is more interested in helping the customer than in anything else. By investing more in the customer in 2001, we can build value in our relationships that will not be easily displaced by a competitor who only wants to win.

Value in production. To a large extent, producing a good product is the science of managing things. To an even larger extent, it is the art of getting the best work out of a myriad of people. To the production manager, nothing counts for more than relationships: a good place to invest in the coming year.

Value at home. Where can we benefit more from accumulated value than with our family? So how shall we invest here? If everyone who depends on us—spouses, kids, cousins, etc.—has more self-confidence as a result of our actions, the value accumulated will be incalculable for everyone. Let's invest in the self-image and self-confidence of everyone around our household this year.

In 2001, let's build value for our future. Let's put more into our relationships than we take out. That way there will be value there, invested, for use in the future.

○ ○ ○

How to Spot a Real Sales Pro

All the parts contribute to the success of the whole.

Integrity exists when a salesperson possesses all the components of success and is able to keep them all functional. Here are the pieces necessary, put into the form of affirmations:

I will not be outworked, out-hustled or discouraged. Marty was the first female salesperson I ever met. (I entered the ranks of young businessmen in the late '50s, and when I started there weren't any women past the job of secretary). She just flat outworked everyone else on the team. She wasn't much on product knowledge or creativity, but she would have been the hands-down winner of the "Use Your Selling Time" award if there had been one. Every available minute of the day when her customers were at their phones or in their offices, she was talking to them or asking for appointments. She did paperwork at night and on the weekends and hit the road every morning. Once, after she had lost her biggest account, she shrugged it off and worked harder on her existing accounts until she had the volume back. Hard work is part and parcel of a winner.

I will listen instead of talk. Great salespeople develop the skill of asking questions. The ability to get people talking about their problems and what they need is the expertise of the best-paid, most respected and happiest salespeople. Ask a question and listen to the answer. Ask another question.

I am undeniable and will make every sale. The really good ones hate to lose ... at anything. My first boss was the worst loser I have ever met. He was incredibly competitive. He wanted to sell everybody everything he could. He measured himself on commission earned, product sold and just how bad he beat his competition inside and outside of the company. A super salesperson is highly competitive.

I will never sell something my customer doesn't need. This is the portal through which many of the people who fail as salespeople enter. "Why do I want to be in sales? Because I really like people and I want to help them solve their problems!" Of and by itself this is not a good reason for being in sales. Companies are full of people who like others and would like to help them, but not all should be in sales for this reason. The best salesman finds out what a customer needs and makes sure he buys it!

I will help build a team. A sales "team" is one of those things where 2+2=5. A salesperson who is helpful, supportive and encouraging to the rest of the group is worth his or her weight in gold. And they will probably earn more, as they can likely expect to be considered for some level of management when the opportunity comes. The No. 1 problem facing management when it comes to generating new management is finding people in their organizations who enjoy helping others achieve their goals. This is what defines good management. A group of salespeople with a great attitude and a sense of team is usually the result of one person's leadership, attitude and help. He who builds a team is incredibly valuable.

Successful selling almost requires the first three characteristics. The last is usually a rare surprise to management. A real sales pro has all.

Wanted: Good Closer!

Many people think there's a big secret to closing a sale.

Everybody liked Harry. As far as his co-workers and customers were concerned, he was a good salesman. He was fun to be around, spent lots of time talking to his clients and would-be clients and was always a positive and cheery contributor at sales meetings. The only problem seemed to be his production. Harry should have been doing better.

Can someone be a good salesman and a bad closer at the same time? Is it possible to have a salesperson who is skilled at almost everything in the sales process merely prime a client for a professional closer? Can someone trained as a "closer" be brought in at the climactic moment to "close the order"? Can someone be a good salesman and a bad closer at the same time?

No! A good salesman is a good closer. A salesperson who is good at everything and unable to close is probably a nice person who ought to find other work or go back to school to learn the whole process.

Harry's manager decided Harry couldn't close. He told him he had better learn how. But what should Harry do to become a complete salesman? Harry wasn't sure what he was doing wrong.

First some questions and then some suggestions:

CLOSING SELF-TEST

Do all your calls start with a goal? The goal can range from getting an order to just getting agreement on some minor issue, just getting acquainted or merely setting an appointment on the phone. But, you can't measure success without a goal.

Are you good at asking questions? Questions have to be asked to uncover what is in the customer's mind. Questions have to be asked without causing resentment and without sounding as if you are conducting a seminar or an inquisition.

Are you tough enough to hang in there until you know if you have achieved the goal you set?

Rate yourself from 1 to 10 on these three items. If you're not happy with your score, here are some suggestions on how to improve:

BECOMING A BETTER CLOSER

Set goals before every sales situation. Before going into a call or picking up the phone, decide what will represent success in that instance, then make up your mind to accomplish the goal. Be realistic. Don't set out to do something that is impossible or unlikely:

The "coup de close." A better word than "close" would be "discover." We've got to find out what the customer is thinking. The best advice is, if there is something you want to know from your client, ask! If you want to know if she is going to buy, ask! If you want to know why he will not be buying, ask! Don't quit until you know what you want to know.

A sales professional is tough enough to keep asking questions (in a pleasant way) until he/she knows everything he or she wanted to find out during the meeting.

Grade yourself. After the call, measure yourself relative to your goal at the outset.

o o o

Salesmanship 501

The path to being the best with your customers, co-workers and leaders

We all have competition. The average buyer of anything has a virtual sea of salespeople calling on him/her (at least as far as they see it), all sounding about the same. The biggest problem our customer faces is sorting all this out and deciding with whom to do business.

The average salesman can expect average results.

In our industry, most buyers have between 20 and 30 salespeople trying to get their business. If I look the same, talk about the same issues, use the same presentation techniques, ask pretty much the same questions, etc., why should I be surprised when I discover I am probably considered an average salesman? By both my company and the client!

The real career-making question is: How can I be different from all these other sharp, educated, trained, eager people? What can I do to stand out, be memorable in a positive, compelling way? I am a believer in asking for the order, but if that's my major selling skill, I am ... average.

Most of our customers must choose products from a list of possibilities presented by you and me and our competition. Therefore, if we have a decent product and aren't totally obnoxious, we can earn an average living.

But how do we excel? What can we do to make our prospects be eager to take our calls, seek our advice and give us more than just a proportional share of their business?

In my first sales job, I started to think selling was all about buying lunches and entertaining my clients. With this technique, I failed miserably.

I decided to become the most technically competent salesman in my territory. No one knew more than I did about our product. Sadly, I was still average in my success.

I remember making a slide presentation (all the hip media presentations of the day were on slides) at an ad agency in Milwaukee and expecting to get warm compliments and maybe even applause when I turned on the lights. Instead I was shocked to discover that my Mr. Big had fallen asleep. Mine had been the third sales pitch made with slides that day. I still was just average.

So, what's the secret?

Sales managers and trainers tell us that we need to get to know our customers' problems. We have to become his/her counselor or adviser. We have to ask a lot of questions.

But I have always felt funny and also understood why it didn't work when I called for appointments saying, "Mr. Big, I'd like to come by and get to know you and your company by asking just a few questions about your business, blah, blah."

What possible benefit was there for a busy Mr. Big in this? Why should he bother to educate yet another would-be salesman?

The goal is for one day to have Mr. Big say, "Pat, we are going to give you the lion's share of our business, but I would like your advice on spending the rest of my budget." When that happens, we have become a real marketing consultant, every salesperson's dream.

So, how does a salesperson reach that dream and become superior instead of average?

That question becomes, "How can I be consistent with my personality, be truly different from the competition, provide consultant-quality service to my customer and get all the business I deserve?"

Think about it. It's career-changingly important to get it right.

Avoid the Lowerarchy

Every group has a hierarchy and, therefore, a lowerarchy. Even a management group.

So, you finally made it to "management land." The promised land. Congratulations! You'll never have to worry again about your job. You're a boss! You're out of the bullpen, into an office! People will now respect you because of your accomplishments, and the pressure to produce will be on your subordinates. All you have to do is get them to work hard and your fame will spread.

Not! Managers, salesmen, accountants, CEOs and every other group has some good ones and some bad. We've all had a bad boss.

My first management job was as sort of a sales manager. There were about 10 others in the company with a similar job, managing salespeople and driving sales. Looking back, I don't think I was very good at it. We were a national company, and my approach as the "new manager" was to travel thousands of miles every week, make calls with the sales team and try to be better with their customers than they were. I saw my job as some sort of super-salesman.

I worked really hard, but I was surely in the bottom half of the group of 10 in my company.

So how do you know if you're in the top half or the bottom half of the class in your company? Here are some thoughts I've picked up the hard way:

Plan: The top-half manager communicates a clear idea of the objective and has a plan that probably was developed by his entire team contributing ideas. Everyone in the group will buy into the plan because they will feel they were part of designing the solution.

The bottom-half manager will be the sole author of the plan and will hand out assignments without ever relating them to the overall objective.

Rewards: The top-half manager sets up a reward system that is part money (mainly because it's an accepted measuring stick and it's the one reward that a person takes home to his or her family) and part recognition given throughout the company, because a good manager knows that money isn't everything.

The bottom-half manager doesn't like to give money or credit. He or she takes most of the credit for success and places blame for failures on the incompetence of the workers.

Leadership: The top-half manager spends the time to find out the career goals of each person working in his group. He realizes that the only way to get a person's best work is to be so obviously interested in the true success of each person that they know the best chance for their own success is to work hard for the success of the manager.

The bottom-half manager probably doesn't know anything about the individuals working for him and their personal goals. If more performance is needed, he just pushes them harder, perhaps offering more money.

Work environment: the top-half manager realizes that family and other personal goals are important to producers. To do the best possible work, producers must feel good about their relationships with others in the company and time spent with family.

The bottom-half manager will push his team to work harder, longer and will not seem to care about anything that happens outside the requirements of production.

Believe that your top management keeps its own pecking order. They know who from their management team belongs in the lowerarchy and are looking for ways to fix it.

o o o

Walking Solutions Are Rare but Unmistakable

We all have a short list of people we would like to "take into battle with us." People we trust, admire and know can solve problems and accomplish objectives.

R ecently, at a seminar, a friend and I were discussing a colleague and what a pleasure it was to be associated with her. She is incredible. When she enters a room, the entire mood seems to get more positive. She has this attitude: "Let's get after the problems here; they are solvable!" and it spreads to everyone involved.

She is realistic, but you have a feeling she will definitely make a difference. She will make something happen. The glass is always half full, and anyone who tends to think differently changes his or her mind or gets left in the dust.

My friend referred to her as a "Walking Solution."

A rare, pleasant, open, insightful, hard-working person who makes you feel that, together, you can make a dent in just about any problem.

What a concept! Somebody in our midst who makes us all function better. How valuable would this person be to your organization?

What would this kind of person be like? Just in case we wanted to identify such a person, or better yet, become one?

My guess at the characteristics:

Cheerful. These people always seem glad to see you and are glad to be "here" no matter what sort of calamity brought the meeting together. They smile and laugh a lot and are generally pleasant to be around. The woman my friend and I were discussing came up to us at the conference, joked a little bit, asked our opinions on the major topic, promised her support and moved on to brighten up the next person's morning.

Get quickly into action. Years ago, as a young salesman I was shocked one morning to find a message from my biggest (and the company's biggest) account informing me that the client was canceling all the business for a year.

I was destroyed! I saw all the negatives, the disaster, the loss of face, the loss of money and the crushing blow to my career.

But a guy in our office who was a "Walking Solution" was not so quick to accept the loss. "Hey, it's not over till it's over," he said. "Let's get on a plane this afternoon and go see them."

They were a whole country away. We made an appointment from the airport, got on a plane, put together a presentation on the plane and at the hotel, saw them the next morning and actually saved the business! The Walking Solution made it a lot easier.

They are quick to take part or all of the problem. "I'll do that!" or "'We can do that!" are what you hear most often from these people. They will listen with intense interest while you describe the problem, often jumping in with questions or suggestions. Then they will come up with a plan that invariably involves them as a participant.

Make others feel good about themselves. It's a knack. The ability, with a few words, to help someone see themselves in light of their strengths. It gives us the little boost of confidence that helps us through tough times and to do things that we were unsure we could do.

Let's pick a week and decide that we are going to be Walking Solutions around our workplaces and homes for that week.

Let's see what effect it has on the people around us, and what effect it has on us.

o o o

The Power of the Employee

If you're like me, you're always looking for ways to make more happy customers. Perhaps the most effective techniques strike closer to home than we think.

It was a meeting where some energetic young folks from AT&T were making a presentation. Afterwards, I was in a group asking questions about what they had done, about AT&T in general and what it was like to work and manage there. The conversation drifted to new ideas in management that were being tried at AT&T. One of the latest and most interesting ideas started with the concept that went something like this: You can't expect any customer to be happier with your product than your employees are with their jobs! Now this is something that makes a lot of sense. I'm not sure where to pass along the credit. Whether the idea comes from some management course or is AT&T home brew, it deserves a lot of thought. It could change the future for many companies.

The best job I ever had while working for someone else was in the mid-sixties at the old Cahners Publishing Company of Boston. I worked in the Chicago office. The reason it was the best job ever was because of the attitude and spirit that was everywhere and in everyone. When I think back, it was a place where we all felt good about ourselves and each other. And we did a lot of business because we knew that we were the best publishing company in the country. Also, as I think back, it was management that was responsible for the spirit in this company. They were tough; they expected results. But they convinced us that we were the "A" team with the emphasis on the word "team." They made calls with us. They wanted our ideas. They gave us credit for a lot of successes. We were rewarded monetarily and psychologically for performance. I was a young salesman, and my management made sure that I learned something new every day. They made sure I worked hard. They enjoyed every victory with me, and they helped me over the mistakes. They also helped me put my mistakes into proper perspective relative to my successes. People who fought the system, people who couldn't survive and be successful in this atmosphere, either quit or were fired. All in all, it was a great place to work. We knew we had the best product, the best management, the best company—and we made sure that all our customers knew it, too.

The worst job I ever had was quite a bit different. I worked for a guy who put his desk up on a platform, elevating himself above everyone else in the room. This elevation extended to most other relationships. His only interest in the team was to be the leader. His ideas were the best, and credit came only after he had siphoned off what he thought was rightfully his. But he wanted the same high level of performance as my former company. Which company do you think got all I had to give?

So, then the question is, if we accept that "You can't expect any customer to be happier with your product than your employees are with their job," what do we do about it?

Make your company a place where people want to work. Demanding, fair, fun, rewarding. Listen to ideas. Give credit where it's due. Most importantly, get to know your employees and their ambitions and dreams. If you want to get the best work that someone has to offer, you must convince them that you are genuinely interested in their future and that you will work hard to help them achieve their goals if you know that they are going to help you reach yours. Tap the true power of your employees by making 1995 the year that they decide that yours is the best company in your industry by a mile.

Find the Time to Be a Good Manager

In part, it means letting others do what you could do more easily. But if you're successful, your business will be stronger. Your people will flourish. And you'll be a better person.

A few years ago, I was based in Boston and I traveled just about every week. I would leave on Monday morning and return Friday afternoon. As the publisher of a good-size trade magazine, I was a very much involved manager. During some weeks, I'd do between 6,000 and 8,000 miles. I felt that I had to attend every major sales presentation. I made calls with a dozen salespeople and visited our biggest customers with a half-dozen writers. I was good; I knocked 'em dead.

But I was never home—and I was a poor manager.

A friend of mine told me the other day, "I'm working harder than ever and we're not making any more money. I never have time to do the things that I want to do. I don't know what is going to happen to makes things better, and I don't know how I will ever get away from this business, because no one up here seems interested in moving up into this job."

If you're really good at a job, or you started a company, how do you get out of the way to train others, to find your successor?

Here's the gist of what some successful managers told me:

Decide you will be a better groomer than a doer. When you really get into it, there is nothing as challenging and as fun as helping someone else grow. Seeing his 10-year-old struggle with a hammer and nail, the father who grabs the tool away and offers to do it probably will wonder someday why his son never developed confidence to match his. More importantly, when his son becomes a man, that father may wonder why their relationship isn't what he had hoped for.

The same principles are at work in the mentoring roles in the business world. If the sales manager makes all the presentations, the salespeople finally will achieve their goals working for another company. If the president sits at the head of the table and makes all the decisions, he'll remain the only person making decisions. If only the CFO explains the great new numbers at the board meetings, odds are the next CFO will be brought in from outside.

The manager who produces even better mangers will enjoy the job infinitely more. Such a manager will have more time to spend doing whatever. Such a manager will be incredibly well liked—and worth a mountain's worth more money than other managers.

Trust your people. You've got to get out of the way. Really. Let them do it their way. Don't be the only one in the group who can have a good idea. All the management books tell you to create an environment where people can make mistakes—but the real trick is to create an atmosphere where people can do it better because they can be themselves. Treat people as if they are going to accomplish more than you ever could. If they believe you, they will.

When we get to be managers, many of us somehow begin to act just a tick smarter, sort of joining in the general expectations that we will be the ones to save the day. Next time your group meets, try this when someone other than the head honcho says something like, "I've got an idea—let's...." Watch to see if everyone, including the speaker, immediately looks at the head honcho, as if silently asking permission to continue. When this doesn't happen, you'll know you're a real manager because people trust themselves.

And more will get done than if you did it all—and you will have lots of time.

You can bring out the leadership in others if they view themselves as leaders. This is true of our employees, bosses, spouses—and certainly our children. To be worthy of the title of manager or leader, we must live this role of helping others catch glimpses of greatness in themselves.

○ ○ ○

Giving Your All

A stunt pilot says, "I leave it all out there every day. I can't do it any better." Can you say the same?

I like air shows. The smell of av-gas, to me, is like the smell of coffee to others. Shiny metal, bright colors and lots of noise all lend atmosphere.

The low-pitched, distinct rumble of a big, radial Pratt and Whitney engine is wonderful music to my ears, and more than one is a symphony. Children, with cherry popsicles dripping down their arms, squint up at the sky and picture themselves at the controls of the jet zooming overhead. Meanwhile, their dads squint in unison, wondering why they never found time to scratch that itch that urged them to learn to fly.

We probably go to a dozen air shows a year. Some of the acts start looking alike and get a little boring. Without diminishing the difficulty of what they do, most of the aerobic acts start to look the same. Air show people call them "flip-flops."

The air shows that are the most fun are in little towns in the boonies. A few weeks ago, we were in Harvard, Neb., for the fifth annual Harvard Air Fair. Four thousand to 5,000 people a day came from miles around to enjoy the airplanes, acts and formations, and food and sun.

One pilot did an aerobatic act that was special. His routine, about twice as long as normal, was one nearly impossible maneuver followed by another, more dangerous and spectacular than the first. He did tail slides, flat spins, lumchevaks (an incredible, end-to-end, tumbling and spinning maneuver), etc. His finale was a stunning demonstration of pure horsepower and skill in which the plane seemed to hang on its prop and nearly hover in front of the crowd.

Later, he sat at a table and signed autographs, mostly for kids. He asked each child his name so he could personalize the signing.

After the line thinned, I told him how much I enjoyed his performance. I said I had been to lots of air shows all over the country and I had never seen anyone better than him.

His response surprised me, but shouldn't have. He said, "Thanks. It's the very best I can do. I leave it all out there every day. When I finish, there is nothing left. I can't do it any better."

I'll bet that guy sleeps better than anybody I know. How many of us can say this to ourselves each day? "There is nothing left. This day I have done my very best."

I had a boss who always said "success comes in cans" (as opposed to cant's). It requires a willingness to extend ourselves mentally and physically beyond where we have been before, to where we can say, "Today, I can't do it any better."

What are some of the management maneuvers we should be doing better? Here are several:

- Practice leadership that gets people promoted.
- Know the professional goals of everyone who works for me.
- Be sure the entire team understands the profit goals of the company.

I'm going to work on these three things until I can honestly say to myself at the end of a day, "I really did these as best as I could. I can't do it any better."

Until now, I don't think I've been able to say about my work what that stunt pilot said about his. But I want to.

Real Sales

When you're trusted by your client, it's easier to be a salesperson.
The hard part is gaining your trust.

How many ways have we heard the joke, "I'm from the ____ and I'm here to help you?" In our society, so many people and institutions claim they are interested only in "helping" us that we become cynical and distrustful any time anyone uses these words. This is particularly true when it comes to salespeople. Everyone distrusts them almost to the point of being hostile at the start.

Walk into a retail store or an auto dealer, and a grinning salesperson will have been programmed to say something like, "Hi, may I help you today?" You then usually say, in response to your own programming born of insecurity and distrust, "No thanks, just looking."

Or how about those people who call us at dinnertime to read to us from their sales scripts. What kind of reception do they get?

Getting beyond this trust barrier is likely the hardest part of sales and the biggest challenge for marketing. We have to do a lot more than just say, "I am a salesman, and I'm here to help you."

We had two young salespeople in our organization who illustrate the point. At the time, one was definitely on the way up while the other was on the way out. Someone observed about the successful one that whatever she did, people connected quickly with her. People picked up right away that she was really going to be a help. Whatever the residual, start-ups resistance, the person's sales personality dissipates it early.

The other half of this example probably had better training, education and experience, but could never get close to his customers. He always seemed to have an artificial pasted-on personality, and people he called on never seemed to get beyond the initial suspicion that we all have for salespeople.

So, is it something you are born with, or can you develop and build the ability to connect with our customers? Our answer would be, "Some of both." Some people come by this ability more easily than others, and you look for it when interviewing. But there are some ways to get better at it.

Be genuine. The thing that you and I detect so easily in others is phoniness. Yet it seems hard for us to detect it in ourselves and quit doing it. Some tactics help us behave more genuinely:

Don't use a script. The worst thing about a script is not that it sounds canned, but that it keeps us from thinking freely and responding from the heart.

Be curious. I was once on a call where we were losing ground, and our man said, "So, I understand that you're not interested today. But before I go, have you sold that property you had listed last month?" They talked for a long time.

Be yourself. If you're not funny, don't tell jokes. If you don't care about the fish on the wall, don't ask.

Talk about something besides your product. Salespeople often come across as being interested only in one thing—selling their product.

Finally, be interesting. If you are not making any headway, if you sense the cold shoulder, don't try to be anything but interesting. For example: Make a bold statement about your product. "We do business with just about all your competitors" is effective.

Ask a question relating to something important to the client. "Would you like to hear more about a new tax saving technique?"

Follow advice from Dr. Spock, author of *Baby and Child Care*. When asked what to do when you just couldn't find the answer to the baby's problem in the book, he replied: "Put down the book, and pick up the baby."

o o o

Know What's Up Before It Goes Down

There's a better way to find hidden hand grenades before they explode.

I once was director of marketing for a fairly large electronics company. I'd been hired to "straighten out the reps" and help the company go direct. Ironically, I was hired because I'd convinced top management I knew something about difficult management situations.

I spent most of the first five or six months in my office, planning and strategizing. I did go into the field a few times to visit reps, but I was more often in the offices of top management.

While I was planning and organizing, the reps were talking and second-guessing. They concluded I was not acting in their best interests, and I never knew it.

KABOOM!!

Needless to say, I didn't do very well in that job, and was gone six months later. I joined the ranks of those who ask themselves every day, "Do I know what's going on right under my nose?"

Our group has discovered several good habits:

Get out of your office. People problems provide the only real grenades in a manager's life. Problems with things can't compare.

Occasionally you can use your office to solve people problems. And then it makes sense when people freely choose that venue.

If the manager chooses his/her office, as in, "See me in my office," it just does not work. What we can almost never do from our office is find grenades scattered throughout our department.

Get out of your office often, and into the flow of what you are managing. Listen to what people are saying. Listen between the lines. Stop and talk to everybody, particularly those you talk to rarely. Be friendly, and see what you get back.

Ask the annual questions more often. Many managers will ask, "How do you like your job?" once a year, at review time. Why not ask once a month? Or more often, if it makes sense? Wouldn't it help to know what's hard, what's easy, who's happy and who's not? You can know a lot just by asking questions.

This must be done honestly. People will give honest answers if they sense the inquirer genuinely cares about the answer and will use it to benefit the one answering.

Be more than a manager, be a leader. The logic is simple but sometimes hard to put into practice: We manage things and lead people. A good leader is genuinely interested in the corporate health and future of his people. As people become convinced you, the boss, really is interested in their future, they will start to trust you.

As you continue to deserve their trust, you will find, almost unbelievably, they become just as concerned about your success and future as you are in theirs.

This should be remembered when we wonder, in our quiet time, about how to be a better manager. People will care about and work for our success as managers in direct proportion to how much we care about and work for their career success.

Let others be part of the idea process. Ask employees, "Here is our problem. What do you think we should do?" If we then can be quiet and listen, it will pay off big, not only in new ideas we didn't think of but also in the trust and cooperation it builds in our team. Once we begin to accept ideas, we will get them from everybody on everything.

Occasionally, we all have to deal with exploding grenades. If we make it our business to know the thoughts and aspirations of everyone on our team, we can go a long way toward minimizing the shrapnel.

○ ○ ○

Do You Talk Too Much?

Most people don't realize the damage they do to themselves when they do.

"Harry, how much time will you need for your part of the presentation?" Harry, a department head with a small company, replied he would need 20 minutes. His fellow department heads rolled their eyes when he wasn't looking because they knew better. Harry could never say in five words what could be stretched to 50. He ultimately took 40 minutes.

It wasn't the end of the world. The work got done. But nobody wanted to spend a lot of time with him. The immediate reason was simple: If you could put a stopwatch on Harry and the rest of the people in a conversation, you would see he did up to 80 percent of the talking.

The negative for his listeners was that they would get bored, tune him out and miss, many times, whatever it was that he had to say. If he were giving a presentation as a middle manager in his company, he would capture his audience in the beginning and lose them by talking two or three times as long as he should.

Harry (under another name) worked for me for a number of years. He was competent in every way except this. The negative for him as a manager was basically that his group members and peers avoided getting into situations where they got cornered and had to just wait him out. Really, no one seemed to think that it was worth talking to him. No one thought it would hurt him professionally; it was just Harry.

But it did hurt him. Somehow he never seemed to make the cut when we were looking for someone to promote. The people in his group often wanted out; that is, when an opening would come up in another department, the upwardly mobile people working for Harry tried to get transferred. I think they were just looking for a better environment.

I tried to talk to him a couple of times. He would shake his head and tell me he realized that he had the problem (he would never say, "I talk too much") and that he would work on it. But it never got any better.

I have failed more than once to be of any assistance to people like Harry.

I came to the conclusion working with him that, often, people who talk too much require more help than can be given by the normal manager.

Another conclusion: When asked to make a point, they will answer beginning with the rationale for the original research ("First, God made the Earth"), then lay out all the facts since then in a very complete way, taking every question as an opportunity to go down yet another lengthy rabbit trail.

Eventually Harry left, looking for greener pastures.

Let me end with this idea: I have never met a businessman who had the reputation for talking too much who also had the reputation for being a fine manager. So you should think about it. Great managers are listeners!

Most people tend to laugh it off ("He's OK. He just talks too much.") But it can be a career killer.

Get help if you need it. Give help if you see it.

Employers of Choice

Good companies spend a lot to find and keep good workers.

Perhaps we could attract better employees if we were better employers. We all spend much time trying to find good employees. We interview, test and re-interview trying to find those who will stick, work, be smart and contribute.

We want people who eventually will grow to replace present management. We need dedicated people, willing to contribute their talents to invent our next generation of products. We need smart people willing to give their working lives to the growth of our company. We try to find the good ones, then get them to commit.

After hiring those we consider good, we train, cajole, promise and reward them, then hope they will stay. We invest much money and resources to keep, motivate, stimulate and encourage them. And still, good people leave.

Perhaps we should consider the problem from the other side. What can we do to be the company of choice? In your business or industry, what would it take to be considered the best place to spend a career? Because that is just what we are asking.

I have a friend whose business is fixing broken companies. These are companies either losing money, not growing, falling apart because of too many family members or failing for other reasons. He's told many stories about the problems he encounters, but one factor seems constant for troubled companies:

"Good people go right through that place," he says. "They stay just long enough to get what they can and they move on. Why don't they stay? What are they looking for? When I get these answers, I will know what is needed to fix this company."

So if your business is the Employer of Choice in your industry, people in your field would know that if they could work anywhere they wanted, they would want to work for you. (You can substitute "Department" for "Employer" and it still follows.)

How can a company earn this reputation? I suspect your list of what's important would be similar to mine.

First is pay: Better people tend to gravitate to the employer willing to pay a little more to get the best.

Trust: Let your key people into the inner sanctum. Better yet, let them help you design it.

Career and growth: Good employees want a clear understanding of what they have to do to get where they want to get professionally. They will go where they can get the best experience and training.

Feedback: The best workers want to know how they are doing. They always will want a dialogue with management.

Contribution and credit: Good employees want to know how they are helping achieve company goals. They will want credit, professional recognition and professional growth for this. An employer of choice will make sure real contributors have a high quotient of self-worth.

Balance: A great company will realize family is important and consider this when making time demands for travel and company business. It is really hard to be happy when your family hates your job for you.

There are other factors worth mentioning. But there is one that, in a way, is more important than the rest. We must treat our key people as important individuals. It doesn't matter how many items we put on a list designed to make us an Employer of Choice. The list will have different meaning for each person.

We will know what motivates people to spend their careers with us after learning their hopes, dreams, aspirations and problems.

To get the reputation as an Employer of Choice, treat key people as trusted, powerful, important individuals.

o o o

Management Short Course: Building People

Somebody challenged me to put everything I believe about management on one side of one piece of paper. Here is a try.

If you want your managers to be hardworking, be sure that you do at least your share of the drudgery.

If you would like your managers to develop self-confidence, help them see themselves in light of their strengths, as they relate to the person they would like to be.

If you would have them be enthusiastic, be excited about them and their projects.

If your people are to be strong enough to make mistakes, tell them about some of yours and how you survived, then help them survive one of theirs and move on.

If you would like your managers to be dependable, discuss *their* problems with them daily; make sure you are in *their* loop; make sure you know *their* priorities.

If you want your managers to make good decisions, discuss *your* problems with them daily; make sure they are in *your* loop, make sure they know *your* priorities.

If you want your managers to be happy, make sure that they make their own decisions.

If you would like your managers to be decisive, always back their decisions.

If you want your managers to be loyal, be genuinely interested in each one's individual success, even if it means that person should leave the company.

If you want them to become sensitive, understanding bosses, don't you ever shout, demean or belittle. Discuss differences and discipline in private. Listen.

If you want your managers to be honest, insist on fair play for all customers and employees.

If you want employees who always give their best work, you will always give them yours.

If you want your managers to come together as a team, make sure that when one is successful, everyone benefits.

If you would have a company with a good sense of humor, remember it's only a way to make a living. It is your job to manage tension along with everything else. Play as a company from time to time.

If you want your managers to be creative, ask for ideas 10 times more often than you give ideas.

If you want your managers to be respected, you must play by the same rules, e.g., get to work on time.

If you want managers to be comfortable in their work, have as many meetings in their office as you do in yours.

If you want to get better performance than you ever thought possible from your managers, believe in them, give them a job and get out of the way!

Real Leaders and Meetings

How effectively do you bring out the leadership in the people who work for you?

Want to know if you're part of a group that has a good leader? Next time you are in a group meeting, watch what happens when somebody besides the boss says something like, "I've got an idea! Let's ..."

Note the reaction. If everyone in the room, including the speaker, hesitates or sort of glances at the boss as if waiting for permission to continue, this group could use better leadership. When this doesn't happen, you know that the management is good because the people trust themselves.

Meetings are a great place to check out ourselves (or other managers) and our ability to bring out the best qualities in others. The group dynamics and individual performances will tell us much about the leadership present.

Meetings can also be a forum for self-aggrandizement by weak managers: "Enough about me, now let's talk about my ideas!"

If this sounds like your manager (or worse, if it sounds like you) at your meetings, you need new leadership assuming that one of the main goals of leadership is to develop new leadership and grow people.

Here's what successful managers have told me:

Use meetings to groom as well as to "do." Every meeting has a main purpose. Make sure that you remind yourself before every meeting that this is a great opportunity to help someone grow and become closer to the person he or she wants to become. This should be the secondary purpose of the meeting. Use the meeting to help get someone ready to do your job.

It's the public-ness of a meeting that makes it so powerful. Positive individual results in a meeting are multiplied by the number of people in the meeting. If you make me feel good about myself in a group of 10 people, I will feel 10 times more reinforced than if it were just the two of us.

More importantly, negative individual results are multiplied by 100 times the number of people in the group. If you make me feel like a jerk in a group of five people, it is 500 times more destructive to me than if it were just the two of us.

So, if you have something bad to tell me, do so in private. In public, ask for my ideas and listen to my answers! Find what you like in what I say and tell me about it. It will help me to trust myself more, and I will have more to give you next time.

Run more interesting meetings. This will generate more participation and more growth from the participants. Everyone will become more comfortable and more involved as time goes on.

Even though the leader must occasionally lay down rules and goals, define responsibility and make specific assignments, the most powerful, uniting words that a real leader can say are, "What do you think?" And then listen.

Some suggestions: Get out of the "power seat" once in a while. Create a schedule in which everyone is assigned to run a meeting. Meet beforehand with this person to make sure his or her experience as the leader is successful. Put others in the power seat. Remember, everyone's ideas are important. Make sure that you get them all. Remember to ask, "What do you think?" Skipping just one person with this question will have a negative effect on the whole team.

Don't let anyone talk too much, and that includes you.

Have an announced time schedule and stick to it. And again, to even begin to think of ourselves as a "leader," we must always be aware of the obligation to help others catch glimpses of greatness in themselves.

Vice President

So you made it to V.P. of your company. So what?
What's the big deal?

First, you can bet that management saw in you a person who sees beyond your primary function in the company. Whether you're the V.P. of finance, sales or production, they will expect you to do that very well indeed, but also to focus on the big picture, with all the problems and all the resources.

Some people, even some employees, think that "profit" is merely a description of what the owners rake off at the expense of the employees and perhaps customers. The V.P. knows that only profit provides continuity for the business and therefore continuity for jobs.

As a V.P. you will be expected to manage dotted lines. Almost anyone can manage the solid-line relationships of boss and worker. It takes a lot more skill in human relations to manage well the interdepartmental problems that exist in all companies. The sales manager fights with production to make more sales. The V.P. (or the one headed in that direction) resolves those conflicts in the best long-term interest of the company. Continuity, profit, jobs, future.

While most workers try to give to their company at least what they get in salary and benefits, some regard the company as a source of paperclips and legal pads for their other projects, and still others view their job as a struggle with some sort of an enemy where you win if you can manage to take our more than you put in. The V.P. understands that the fiscal and psychological health of the "company" is at least as important as that of any individual in the company. That the company can do the most good for the most people, owners and employees alike, when it is financially healthy and the workers are happy with the work. He or she welcomes the challenge this presents.

A V.P. knows that the most important resource is the people. A V.P. has learned that the only important secret of being a good boss is to be genuinely interested in the welfare of each individual employee. He or she knows how hard this is to achieve and also that if every employee in the company knew that someone in management was sincerely interested in his or her success, this company would soar ahead in its ability to out-think and out-produce the competition.

The saying goes "the buck stops" at the top man or woman. But a good V.P. makes sure that it stops at his or her desk first if at all possible. V.P.s are good flak absorbers. Actually, they enjoy the feeling that comes with meeting a problem, understanding it and handling it.

A good V.P. knows the value of a "no surprises" environment. Everyone knows what is happening and where they fit into the picture. The V.P. and his or her boss know that they will never surprise each other. The V.P. expects and gives the same consideration to the people who report to him or her. This all takes a great deal of commitment to communications.

V.P.s have plans and goals. They expect their bosses and employees to have them too, and express them.

They understand the culture of the company. They are able to see across the barriers and blockages between departments and are able to organize and unite the best people to get the job at hand completed in the best interest of the company.

The title of V.P. is more than a reward for running a department well; it is a challenge to do even more. The job has no hours, only commitment. Commitment to quality of the product, loyalty to the mission of the company, commitment to the growth and fulfilment of every individual in the company … and to making a profit.

○ ○ ○

Argentina!

The people of Argentina make it a great place to visit and to do business.

Last month I went to a soccer game in Argentina. The game was to be huge! The winner would advance to the final four of the South American Cup. It was going to be between Velez, the champion of the Argentine league, and America, the top Mexican team.

People streamed in, probably some 50,000 when all was said and done. It was taking place in a suburb of Buenos Aires. We had beautiful seats about 30 rows up, just about center field. There was an air of excitement that even we gringos who didn't understand the game could feel. It was going to be a night to remember.

We went to the game in a small bus that I think was hired by the hotel. There were five gringos in our group. As my wife Janet and I sat down, I noticed a couple of kids across the way who we learned later were 8 and 10 years old. The two seats in front of us were vacant, and it didn't take these kids long to get into them, hang off the backs of the chairs facing us, and begin to try out their English. They were in grammar school and they could speak English well enough so that we could have a meaningful conversation.

We found out all about them, their families and their school.

We introduced ourselves to their parents and, through hand signals, bad Spanish and returned poor English, we got along. The interesting thing was that we could communicate better with the youngsters than with their parents. I tried to imagine which of my own grandchildren would have had the same presence, charm and presentation to go up to strangers who spoke Spanish and try to have a conversation with them.

Just a few years ago Argentina was a dictatorship. These kids and many others from Argentina will shape a much different future for their country, claiming their rightful place on the world stage.

Back to the stadium!

The soccer was sensational! Fast, skilled and hard fought. The home team won 2-0, thus earning the right to represent Argentina in the final four of the South American Cup.

Some interesting things happened that one would never have seen at a National Football League game. The crowd (very, very partisan) never stopped singing, waving flags and cheering for an hour and a half. At times they jumped up and down in unison so vigorously I thought at one point they might actually damage the stadium. The song was a simple "battle hymn" that went something like, "C'mon Velez, c'mon, c'mon! When Velez plays, we are here and Velez will win!" All the time standing and pushing one or both arms forward as if to say, "Forward, onward!" For an hour and a half.

And a number of times during the game a huge flag was unrolled in the end zone (where most of the action was, similar to the South Stands at Broncos games) from row one to the very top of the stadium. But this flag must have covered 4,000 fans! Such cooperation! After more loud cheers it was rolled back from the top to the bottom, leaving it perfectly placed for the next time. Incredible!

They had a sort of moat and a high fence between the field and the crowd, probably reflecting previous problems. There was a plastic passageway that allowed the players to take the field without being subjected to the wrath of the home crowd. They served no alcohol at all, and it seemed that they had crowd control pretty well figured out, perhaps even better than we do.

The young man who drove our bus told me not to cheer for Mexico or we would be thrown down to the field by the fans. But right in front of us a man cheered loudly for the Mexicans and he was left alone, given respect.

Ironically, while we were in Patagonia there were protests against President [George W.] Bush, who was attending the South American Summit near Buenos Aires. In discussing it with locals, I got the impression that they more or less separated politics from everyday life. They don't care much for Bush, but they don't seem to connect the people of the U.S. with him. They don't see politicians anywhere acting on behalf of the people as much as in the politicians' own interests.

Everywhere I went in Argentina, including the soccer stadium, I found helpful, intelligent people. The kind of people I would like to spend time with, the kind of people that I would like to do business with. These people, I think, will be in our future.

o o o

Adversity

Growth, and even life, can't take place without it.

Once, at a sales meeting, I asked a group of about 39 journeymen salespeople, "How many of you have a story that begins with, 'Let me tell you about the day I almost quit.'?"

As far as I could tell, everyone in the room raised his or her hand. So I asked a few to share their stories. It was fascinating because they were all people I knew well, and yet I had never heard most of the stories they told me.

One man who was successful in both sales and management shared that after about six months of getting put down and beat up as a "newbie," he was ready to quit. He even had his goodbye speech memorized to his boss. But for some reason, his boss quit first.

So the man with the goodbye speech reconsidered, figuring there was a new opportunity at that company. He made up his mind that he would give it six months and work harder than ever to be good at it. He did work harder. And he became good at it. I know he looks back at that time as a trying period—and a turning point in his career.

A woman told of how the only thing that kept her in what she, after two months, thought was a job she couldn't do, was the deal she made with her boss in the beginning to give it one year. She is now one of the most successful salespersons and managers in her field.

My own beginning in sales was quit shaky. In my second sales job (my first ended in failure) I remember vividly a training session on making telephone cold calls. I remember it vividly because it was probably the most embarrassed I have ever been. We were a group of about 10 new salesmen. It was my turn to make cold calls out of the Yellow Pages while everyone else listened in on extensions.

We had a track to use as direction. I was talking "track" with a guy out of the phone book, but I ran out of "track." I didn't know what to say or where to go, so with every one of my contemporaries listening, I just hung up!

Total collapse, total humiliation. The only reason I stayed with the company was that I didn't want to fail again. I wanted to do it right. And I eventually did.

My daughter works with handicapped skiers at Snowmass. These are the veterans without legs or arms or eyesight who careen down mountains on one ski or a sled, some using only the voice of a guide to make their way. They love what they do, and they do it with a passion and abandon and they are successful because of their attitude about adversity. This year they presented my daughter with the following line as their creed:

Life is not a journey to the grave with the intention of arriving in a pretty and well-preserved body, but rather to skid broadside, totally used up, thoroughly worn out, and loudly proclaiming, "Wow, what a ride!"

Some version of this is probably the modus of most successful people.

Take chances, expose your confidence and decorum to possible failure, stick your neck out into unfamiliar places.

Live! And life will come to you!

A Management Migraine

Lessons in communication from mushrooms.

As I write this, I'm on my way to a Central American country to help friends change out some management. And when I say "change out" I mean we are trying to fix a disaster and get restarted on a new course. The sad part is that I was one of the people who got this particular disaster started in the first place.

I am on the board of this small outfit (it has about 50 employees), and I was one of the people who interviewed the man we hired as director of our enterprise. The first year everything seemed to proceed at a good pace.

Now, at the end of our second year, we have totally blown the year. All our production numbers are down; all our expense numbers are up. Almost everybody who works there is unhappy and finger-pointing. It is not a pleasant place to work.

Now we have the resignation of an angry director who thinks he was not given the right chance and the proper tools, and he mostly blames the incompetence of the people working for him. We have a workforce that is totally dispirited, claiming to be without direction and leadership. And we have a board scrambling to find a new director, reinvigorate a workforce and get back on track.

A real Board Headache.

We'll get it fixed. We have good leads already on a new director, and, of course, we have our work cut out for us in motivating the workers. But we will get it done.

I think it's important to discuss what happened and why. The basic problem was, as they say in the military, "a failure to communicate." It turns out the boss, the guy we hired to be the leader, never talked to members of his team except to give an order or to find fault. To him this was communicating. He was, however, extremely knowledgeable in the industry. He knew what he was trying to get done; he just couldn't get it to happen.

I remember being told in the beginning when we were interviewing, that in Central and South America the workplace culture was different. The bosses were tougher and more dictatorial, and the workers were used to just doing what they were told, no questions asked. They were happy to have a job. Even so, we quizzed all applicants on their people skills, but this one got through our filter.

I never really accepted the idea that you could get high performance from people you treat like mushrooms (keep in the dark and sprinkle with fertilizer once in a while), and I would use this instance as evidence to support my opinion. But even in a culture where mushrooms do the work, you would think that it wouldn't take very long for management to discover that these "shrooms" are really people in disguise, and if we treat them as such it will result in incredibly better performance. Certainly a lot better for the guy who is now losing his job.

But the board of directors was the biggest culprit in this case: The board should have had a connection with this manager instead of waiting a year and a half before finding out what happened.

The director was a good man with a lot of industry knowledge and should have been helped by the board to be a better manager. In a very real sense we did the same thing to the director that he did to the workers: We shroomed him. What we should have done is obvious.

Anybody you mushroom will perform poorly. Think about it.

Put Down the Book and Pick Up the Baby!

Everything you need to know about selling, on one sheet of paper.

If you sit down over a beer and ask a salesman or saleswoman how it's done, they will pretty much all tell you the same thing. They will say that a top salesperson gets to be very good friends with his customers, helps them solve their business problems and therefore is very much on the inside when it comes time to buy. It's not that you get something for nothing, it is that somehow you have earned the right to have a chance at the business.

I always had a goal that went something like this: When my customers got to know me I wanted them to say, "Pat, we are going to use your products this year as you have probably guessed, but I want your advice on how to spend the rest of my budget on the things we have been talking about all year."

Now, I didn't always get this, but having it as a goal kept my mind on the target of "just how can I help this guy." It helped me limit the times I made the worst mistake that salespeople make, and that is talking incessantly about myself and my product. Many of us don't realize just how boring and how damaging it is to our cause.

Most of us know we should be spending most of our time trying to help our customers solve their problems, not telling anyone who will listen how great we are and how incredible our products are.

So here comes the biggest problem that salesmen face:

What if you don't know the client? How do you say, "If you will just let me into your inner circle today I'm sure I can help you make some good decisions." Or, "I know more than you think I do."

It is very difficult to earn the right to be someone's friend! The best advice I can give I got 40-some years ago from a book I had to read because we were having kids. It was *Baby and Child Care*, by Dr. Benjamin Spock. I think we wore out three of these books because we had a lot of kids. But one day I read somewhere that Spock had written, "There comes a time to put down the book and pick up the baby!"

So when you're making cold calls or calling on people you don't know very well, forget about sales theory; truly try to help your client and try to be different than all the other salesmen you have heard. (When your customer hears a line he has heard from some other salesperson who has disappointed him, you're toast!)

So here are my rules. It is not easy. But that is why sales is usually a high-paying job if you're good at it.

First, you must be quick to ask a question. Every time it is your turn to talk (like right after Mr. Big says hello) you must ask a question within 10 seconds.

Second, you must avoid talking about your product (because that's what everybody else does). Best is to make a statement about his/her business and then throw it back to him/her with a question. Like, "I understand that you compete with Acme. Have you seen their latest ads?"

When he/she starts explaining things, keep asking questions until you learn something. Leave, gather more info, come back again, try and learn more. Occasionally you will have the opportunity to explain your product, but over time you will earn the right to be a consultant to your customer.

There are a few good salesmen. Customers are looking for them.

○ ○ ○

Secrets of the Oracle of Delphi

There is very little new under the sun.

In ancient Greece, there were a couple of interesting careers which we don't have available to us anymore. At least in the same form.

I bring them up now because they offer modern-day lessons in life, and because my wife and I learned about them during a recent vacation trip to Turkey, Greece and the Greek islands, enabling us to cross off one of the top 20 items on our lifetime wish list.

The first career was that of runner. There just was no easy way to get information from one place to another. Many towns built towers on which the townspeople would start fires to warn the next group down the line of oncoming danger. But the most common way of communicating was through the runner.

When an unexpected boat docked in Piraeus, someone fleet-footed ran to Athens with the news. Only the swift and fit could make a career out of running, but those who did were well paid and an admired group in the Greek culture, often called on to do heroic service for their country.

When the Phoenicians invaded Greece in 490 B.C., they did so along the north coast, at a town called Marathon. After the Greeks managed to defeat the Phoenicians, they sent a runner 29.2 miles to Athens with the news. He ran as fast as he could. When he reached his goal he managed to say, "We won the battle!" Then he collapsed and died.

A heroic effort. Yet later, it wasn't the messenger who was remembered in the naming of an Olympic event, but the town from which he ran! That's one lesson.

The other impressive career path from antiquity was that of an oracle. An oracle was a "seer," one who could give advice, tell the future and get paid in return. A common behavior for would-be oracles was to go barefoot in order to more clearly pick up vibrations of future events passing through the earth.

The most successful and well-known oracle was the priestess of Apollo called Pythia, who was located at Delphi. The ruins at Delphi today indicate that this oracle was successful indeed. Kings and princes from all over the world came to Delphi for advice and in return poured incredible riches into her treasury.

Reportedly she would ask questions, listen and then enter some sort of trance from which she would offer insightful advice and clues to the future. For example, after some conversation and discussion with Alexander the Great, she told the ruler, "Young man, you are invincible!"

Alexander then went out and conquered the entire world of that time. That's lesson No. 2. It sounds to me like the oracle was the first effective business consultant. She asked, listened, discussed and finally was able to tell people what would be their best strategy. And she filled her treasury to overflowing without doing anything, outside of providing advice.

Ever since the visit, I have been on the lookout for a consulting firm that calls itself Delphi Consulting. Seems a company by that name would really be worth listening to.

It probably would have a division called Oracle Management Training, where they teach businesses how to listen to and understand their employees, then help the employees see themselves in light of their strengths, so they, in turn, have the self-confidence to build their careers.

It probably would have another division called Oracle Sales Management. Here it would teach: "Listen to your customers until you know enough to help solve their problems. Your customer then, almost magically, will buy your product."

Incidentally, during my visit, I asked the oracle what I could do to improve myself.

She quickly told me I was just right, and not to change a thing.

o o o

Just Another Board Meeting

Business and capitalism can help a lot in tough places

We were sitting in a barnyard, on those plastic chairs that nest together and cost about four bucks apiece at Target. Someone had brought them in a pickup truck. There was a huge pig, chased by a half-dozen barefoot, bare-chested kids. Numerous dogs, chickens and cats joined in the fun, while a beautiful macaw perched on a fencepost and made a big ruckus when one of the kids occasionally swiped at it with a stick. On the other side of the fence, cows grazed peacefully.

Everyone was asked politely if they wanted to use the outhouse facilities before our meeting started. A few did, and remarked to our hostess how clean they were. Things settled down, and the focus shifted to our circle of about 10 people. We were in a small village in rural Honduras, about an hour from La Ceiba. The board meeting was about to begin.

A few years earlier, after Hurricane Mitch, I had flown to Tegucigalpa, Honduras, with some friends, in a DC-3 loaded with medical supplies. While working with the Dole Food Co. to secure a place to park our plane, I got acquainted with a very interesting young man named Tony Stone.

Tony grew up in Honduras, graduated from Stanford as an aeronautical engineer, worked in the U.S. aerospace industry as a rocket scientist for 10 years and then returned to his home country. He and his new lawyer wife, fellow Stanford grad Kim Walsh Stone, committed to give a minimum of five years to helping rebuild after the destruction of Mitch.

A couple years ago Tony and Kim started the Adelante Foundation, which does micro-lending to the very poor in Honduras. They lend small amounts of money (about $100 to $200) to very poor rural women who then buy something (sundries, a pig, etc.) as the beginning of a business. They repay the loan from profits over three months and usually borrow more as their business grows. It is a self-help system that really works. One of the women, for example, borrowed to buy a used popcorn machine, and now makes enough to pay down her loan and about $15 profit per week, selling sacks of popcorn in her village. In Honduras, $15 can be a decent month's pay. Now, she can think about more school, better food and clothes for her kids.

Back to the board meeting. The women who borrow money from Adelante are formed into groups of women who know each other. They are individually and collectively responsible to repay. This way they help each other and depend on each other. So far Adelante has more than 70 loans out and up to now has a 100 percent repayment record.

Honduran women are becoming an economic force in their communities. Each woman in turn talked about what had happened since the last "corporate" visit; how they spent their money, whether sales were good or bad, what they needed to do a better job, etc.

A number had recently completed repaying their previous loan. When asked how much they would like to borrow this time, they would smile and say that they wanted more than they thought they could get because they realized that the more goods they could buy, the more profit they could make. The smiles said more than a million words about how they understood how a little capitalism could help them and their families.

We asked if there was competition. They said yes, and this generated quite an interesting conversation about customer service, pricing and getting good help.

We were all totally drawn into the discussion being led by these four women (whose formal education probably averaged five years each). They said that they were outselling their competition because they were more focused on customer service and they were priced right. It occurred to me that we could have had the same conversation sitting in the boardroom of Coca-Cola.

No one will ever be able to measure the effect of this program on the GNP of Honduras, but it will affect many people and many families. Although it isn't the source of all answers, business and capitalism have a lot to offer for the solution of the world's great problems.

o o o

Success Lies in the Big Picture

Want to see more success? Then see more of what's around you!

You hear it all the time when you're watching football on TV.

Just a couple of weeks ago a pair of sportscasters who always sound the same no matter who they are or what game they're covering were discussing why Rich Gannon of the Oakland Raiders was not only the best player on the Oakland team but also the rightful winner of the Most Valuable Player award this season in the NFL.

The two were saying that even though Gannon has some of the best quarterbacking skills (but not the best), his true genius is in the way he can see the entire field of play.

Most quarterbacks, they said, make millions simply because they can execute well-practiced routes and plays. Gannon can do all that, too.

But he can also innovate because he has the rare knack of instinctively knowing not only where everyone on his team is and where they will be, but also just what the defense will do about it.

He is much more valuable than most because he sees his job, the team goal, the individual goals of each of his teammates and how they all interconnect.

People who can see the big picture in business are also worth their weight in gold.

Too many people think they are moving toward the next rung on the ladder when they don't even know what they would do if they were standing on it.

What kind of people is your management looking to promote? People who, among other things, are great at their own jobs but who at the same time understand the team goal and even the company goal? And people who do something to help everyone accomplish each one's individual part?

If you are a dynamite salesperson, you can continue to make a great living doing what you are good at for as long as you wish. If you want to someday be a sales manager, however, you should do things a little differently.

You should become sensitive to the goals and problems of your fellow salespeople, and spend some time helping them achieve what they want to achieve. In other words, start doing things for the company that demonstrate your ability to see the entire playing field, not just the competition that exists on the route you are running.

Don't do the following unless you want to be considered for a bigger job in your company:

Become sensitive to the bigger picture. If you are not sure what happens on the next rung or the one beyond that, ask. Nothing will be more interesting to you if you are sincere. And nothing will be of more interest to your boss than an employee's genuine concern for what really makes the company tick.

Contribute beyond your own job. Management is crucially interested in finding people who show an aptitude for understanding the company mission and how to achieve it. Be interested, make suggestions and extend a helping hand without worrying about extra compensation. What comes around, goes around.

Help others succeed. If you don't remember anything else from this, remember that the hardest person for management to locate is the person who enjoys helping others be successful. Make it your hallmark to help others in your group achieve their goals.

Proud to Be a Peddler!

Or anything else you want to call someone who can sell and market! From the Flintstones to dot.com, the good ones have been in great demand.

I used to be offended by the words "peddler" and "pitch." But no more. I don't use them myself. I think that people who do are trying to put suede shoes on someone who is really wearing work boots, and who has the talent and ability required to do something they don't quite understand.

Occasionally I go on sales calls with our people. I really enjoy doing it because it's where the fun is and where the energy comes from in our business. Probably our salespeople think my main purpose is to see if they are performing up to par. But my real reason is to try to absorb some of the energy that exists only at the point of attack. At the point where it all begins when it comes to business success.

This one customer, after deciding to buy a six-issue program in one of our magazines, was surprised when our salesperson began telling him how much better his marketing program would be if it were nine or 12 issues. He smiled broadly and said, "You peddlers are all alike, always trying to get me to buy more than I want to buy." The problem was, he didn't want to buy enough to solve his marketing problem. Our job was to help him solve his problem completely.

It's hard to be good at selling. Work ethic, personality and insight are important, as in all jobs, but being good at selling requires a weird balance between the desire to help others and the will to win for yourself, to stand out and achieve. Everything you do (or don't do) is out front and measurable. Everyone in the company (probably in the industry) knows how well you are doing. So, most successful salespeople have an ego and self-confidence that relishes the visibility, and are motivated by it.

But the really great salespeople solve problems. Other people's problems. This requires getting out of the limelight. Or better yet, it means putting your customer in the limelight. Honestly and permanently. All the modern sales training courses aim at becoming a "counselor" or "advisor" to the customer.

Some of the "type A" people who go for sales have a hard time relinquishing the pedestal and replacing "me" and "I" talk with "you" talk.

But when you find one who really enjoys helping others, and also has a lot of drive to be personally successful and the self-confidence not to be intimidated by Mr. Big, then you have the combination that will win.

As an industry average, each salesperson in the United States generates business that 50 workers depend on for jobs. Very few (I know of none) businesses can exist by simply waiting for the phone to ring. In publishing we help people grow their businesses, but we would die if we waited for them to figure it out and call for help!

Even the dot.coms get it. Awash in investor money, they are pouring it into television and magazine advertising, trying to drive you and me to their websites. Even the Internet can't work without marketing and sales. As a recent article in *USA Today* points out, "Pocket protectors are out, marketing skills are in at tech start-ups." They may have a lot of money to begin with, but they will merely spend it if they don't sell enough product to have a profit.

In our case, we don't make magazines, we solve marketing problems through advertising. Years from now we will be doing the same thing in who-knows-what media.

The fondest of my business memories are of stand-up presentations in boardrooms full of important people not really ready to believe what we were about to say. Where you had to know who you were selling as much as what you were selling, being good on your feet counted; you had to be ready to face the devil himself, and huge chunks of business hung in the balance.

Nothing happens until something is sold.

This will never change. I am proud to be one of the foot soldiers.

○ ○ ○

Balance

Watch out! Success will come from where you are focused.

Strangely, I've known two people in my life who have given up just about everything else to be champion skeet shooters (shooting clay pigeons with shotguns). One guy in particular practiced every day, seven days per week, shooting at least 500 shells per day. He became a national champion, but that's about all he became.

In business it's about the same. Years ago, we were in a different business and had a partner who helped our company a lot. But he had only one major focal point: money and the generation thereof.

He would often say, "A company must generate value for the stockholders." As you might guess, he was the major stockholder.

Of course, all businesses must generate value for their stockholders or the businesses will find themselves without investors. But if money is the only motivator, the result will not be a very good business.

That partnership started out pretty well, with its concern for stockholders matched with other concepts like importance of people, work environment, job satisfaction, growth potential, etc.

But after some years, everything else took a lower place to "my money" for this man. He ended up with more than his fair share of the money while losing friends and respect. As we consider who we want to be in business and in life, it is worthwhile to think about what demands are being made on us by the people around us. And then ask ourselves what is important to us and what is not. Effective people find a way to balance the needs of all the influences in their lives:

Managers: They look to us to perform and to help build the company. They measure things like profit, sales, leadership skills and whether we can lead a team, grow and develop good people, etc.

Employees: They look to us for leadership and opportunity. They measure us on things like training, opportunity for growth, understanding, respect, sense of team, etc.

Customers: They look to us for solutions to their problems. They measure our performance on the basis of our ideas, solutions, honesty, service, fair prices, etc.

Family: Maybe most important, our families look to us for a good family life. They measure things like how many soccer games we get to, whether we spend enough time with them to know them and help them be successful, and whether we're supportive, present, caring, etc.

How can you be a good manager if all you are interested in is the bottom line? How can you be a good salesman if you don't really know your customer, or if you don't try to help your fellow salesmen? How can you be good at anything if you don't give your family as much time as it deserves?

The most valuable persons sought by management and the rarest are those who can get out of their own way and grow other people. Much is asked of the person who wants to be effective.

Probably too much.

But the people we follow and enjoy being around do a pretty good balancing act. Perhaps we should do better.

There's Nothing Like Cash

There is no more important item to a successful business. You can have profit and money, but without cash, you have nothing.

We were sitting around our conference table, six teachers from Denver high schools and six of our managers. It was part of the Denver School-to-Career Partnership Program and was designed to improve communication between business people and teachers. The overall goal was to reach their students.

We were occupied with nervous, get-acquainted small talk when somebody asked about the sign hanging near the office of our accounts receivable manager. It says, "A Sale Is a Gift Until the Money Is Collected."

We talked a bit about words and business.

"What's the most important word in business?" a publisher asked. A short chorus from the teachers: "Profit," said one. "Customers," said another. "Sales." "Quality." "Money."

We agreed each is important. But there is something without which there can be no business. More conversation, and then, "Cash!" cried the most outspoken teacher, really getting into the swing of it.

"Isn't that the same as money?" someone asked.

"No," said a teacher who had been quiet until then. "There are all kinds of money that you can't spend. Cash, you can spend."

"You're right," said another. "Like stocks, bonds, checks, promissory notes and even promises. None of these spend like good old-fashioned cash."

"Why is cash important to the point that it takes precedence over things like sales and profit?" I asked.

Everyone thought for a beat, and then the thoughtful, quiet one declared, "Because cash is the only thing that you can use to pay bills, give raises, invest in research or hire new people, just to mention a few uses." Nods of agreement all around.

A spirited and more surprisingly positive conversation ensued about the importance of profit turning into cash so a company has something to spend. They all agreed you can't spend profit.

"I can't believe we are sitting here having this conversation," one teacher said. She was asked why.

"It has just never seemed appropriate to talk about money, profit and cash this way. It's just not been something that teachers concern themselves about. We try to teach kids a little bit about handling money, but the importance of generating cash and profit ... well, it just wasn't our job."

"What do you think now?"

"We should do more of it."

"Let's take this one step further," I said. "Who pays teachers?"

"The schools."

"Where do the schools get this money?"

"From the government and taxes." I could tell they still didn't see where I was going.

"Where does the government get the tax money?"

Sensing the trap was related to business, someone said, "from individuals who pay taxes."

"And where do the taxpayers get the cash to pay their taxes?"

"From their jobs."

Before I could close my little trap, they all seemed to jump in willingly when one said, "Which, of course, means that if companies don't have profits and cash, then teachers won't teach, workers won't get raises, government won't get taxes, charities won't be funded and you wouldn't have the time or resources to sit here with us and discuss the issues."

Cash and profit are not bad words. They are critical concepts to the success of our economy.

o o o

The Most Potent Management Tools of All

Words: We can do more damage and more good with them than with anything else.

I tried out for the high school football team as a sophomore. Through grammar school, I caught passes and helped teams win. I felt pretty good about myself. This was my chance to make my young man's dreams of athletic success come true.

An assistant coach handling the would-be receivers put us through a number of drills. They consisted mostly of running from an imaginary line of scrimmage and then cutting sharply to one side in time to try to catch his pass.

Well, he had an arm like John Elway and I was really nervous. The football arrived in a blur, like a rocket, just as I turned to look for it. Each time I missed it, I got more flustered and less coordinated. Though the coach seemed to snicker disgustedly, I knew I'd get it timed right in just a minute.

That was until this young assistant shouted to me across the field— loaded with people I longed to impress—"Wiesner (mispronouncing it WIZENER), you'll never be a football player 'cause you can't catch s---!"

I might as well have worn catcher's masks on my hands for the rest of that practice. I was cut that day. I quickly went from knowing I could be an effective football player to knowing I never could be.

Years later, as a young man starting in business, I gave a presentation for the first time to a room full of peers. I was scared to death. Afterwards, my boss told me just how good a job he thought I had done. He told me in such a way that I knew he really believed it.

I can remember his exact words and see the expression on his face 35 years later. I never had the same depth of fear in these situations again. I've often recalled his encouraging words to get me through personal difficulties.

You'd think those of us who manage others would develop a sense of the power of our words. But we don't always.

I sat in a manager meeting in which the company president weekly picked somebody to almost destroy. One week he told the chief engineer,

"Any dumb SOB knows that a good design needs to be maintainable, but not our chief engineer!"

Another time he told Marketing, "If we paid you by the good marketing idea, you'd starve!"

All this and more in open court. This company had great products but people didn't stay long.

How many times have you or I done the business management equivalent of saying to our child, "Give me that hammer. You don't know how to pound a nail"?

A bigger question: After you have taken a bite out of someone's self-image, how hard is it to repair the damage? One expert claims it takes 20 positive statements to offset one negative remark.

If you tell me my ideas and writing are terrible (or tell your kid he/she is dumb, or tell your spouse that any jerk can understand the computer), you will need to expend 20 times the effort to bring my (their) self-image back to where it was before you passed judgment.

There are a number of people in our companies and among our families and friends who care very much what we think. We can do a lot of damage or a lot of good, depending on how we talk to them.

How Does Tiger Do It?

What can we do that Tiger Woods does to make us better?

At a cabin in the mountains, looking for something to read on a rainy day after having watched Tiger Woods win yet another big tournament on TV, I picked up an old (May 2002) copy of *Reader's Digest* and started to read an article written about the then-indomitable Woods, condensed from an issue of *Newsweek* in 2001. The author, Devin Gordon, asked why Woods was virtually unbeatable, and the question was discussed using examples of other sport "dominators" of the day, like Martina Navratilova, Reggie Jackson and Wayne Gretzky. Here's what they thought, along with some thoughts on what we might take from their examples to do our jobs better.

Genius is 99 percent sweat. Hard work and preparation is a key to success in every human endeavor. Martina Navratilova has said, "For every good shot one makes, they have hit a thousand in training." Tiger Woods is well known for constantly, incessantly hitting practice balls.

A valuable businessperson works hard. Usually success is directly proportional to the "hard." When building a team in a business, the team leader cannot expect more work and dedication from members of the team than he/she gives.

Make your competition nervous "by appearing relaxed," says Gretzky. Be competent and cool, say the athletes. Make it look easy. Your competition will make mistakes.

In business, we build confidence and coolness by building a sense of team. If our team is confident in our product, energized by their teammates and doing an outstanding job for the customer, then they will surely be respected by the competition.

Don't just dominate, intimidate. Woods doesn't want to merely win the most tournaments; he wants to win the biggest and the best. He thus puts the most pressure on himself and his competitors. His competitors say to beat him you have to play without errors.

The only way to dominate and intimidate our business competitors is to do things big, do things right, be creative and serve our customers better than ever. At the same time, we develop a sense of team in our people that makes them want to perform at the highest level. When the team performs at the highest level it becomes an undeniable force in the market.

Never be satisfied. Tiger was the best in 2002, and he is the best today. Yet he still works harder on his game than just about any other golfer. Chris DiMarco, who lost a dramatic playoff to Woods in the 2005 Masters, said, "He has different objectives than I do. My principal goal is to win money to support my family. His is to win every tournament."

I would bet that many of Woods' competitors say that.

If our business team is convinced that as a team we can always do better for the customer and for each other ... we will!

The article didn't mention it, but it probably all started with Tiger being born with an incredible athletic ability. Yet even that would have gone to waste or at least fluttered in mediocrity without the crushing work and preparation that Woods has put into being the best he could be. We are all gifted in life to one degree or another. The real test is what we make of ourselves from the raw material.

Lombardi Salesmanship

Do you know salespeople in need of food for thought? Try these morsels from the old coach.

An old friend, recently retired and without question one of the best salesmen I have ever known and a collector of interesting sales techniques, sent me a copy of an old Vince Lombardi videotape called "Second Effort." As everyone knows, Lombardi was coach of the Green Bay Packers football team during a time when they were invincible, early in the days of the newly formed National Football League. I suppose someone convinced him that his football ideas were transportable to other fields and that he would be more famous (and more rich) if he made a videotape.

The tape has to be at least 25 years old. I promised I would look at it, but as I put it into my VCR, I found myself feeling a little annoyed at having to do so. As the credits came on (Dartnell Press), you could tell that this was a really old piece (Jerry Kramer looked 25 years old), and I wondered just how far back in the dust we had left old Vince Lombardi's ideas on selling.

Well, you guessed it. The coach had some really good answers that not only apply now as well as then, but will apply until the last item available is sold. For example:

Commitment: As you might expect, Lombardi used football to illustrate his point. In any given game, he said, there are about 140 plays from scrimmage. But only about three of these plays in each game turn out to be important enough to influence the final outcome. The problem is that, because no one knows which three plays will be the ones that will turn the tide, the players must be prepared mentally and physically to go all out in all 140 attempts. Those who aren't ready to do this fail. In Lombardi's words, "They can't be a Green Bay Packer!" Well, in selling, if you aren't ready to go all out every day, all day, you will fail. "You can't be a salesman!" because you won't be working at full tilt when the hidden opportunity comes your way.

Study your competition: He tells how, after every game, every one of those championship players would sit and analyze their opposite number for that game. In sales, he says, you should know not only your own product, not only your competitor's product, but also your competitor's company and, most importantly, the person who is selling directly against you. Know their habits and techniques and how they sell. What do they talk about? How often do they make calls? Only in this way will you know what it is that you must do to be better.

Prepare: You might expect the coach to tell us to get physically in shape for both football and selling. He does just that, pointing out that "fatigue makes cowards of us all." In addition, know your product and the wonders it can do for your prospects just as well as the champion Packers knew how to block and tackle.

Second effort: Win! He did, in fact, say, "Winning isn't everything. It's the only thing!" Because losing games doesn't do anything for the Packers, and losing sales doesn't put food on your table or cars in your garage or even feathers in your cap. With a lot of neat football footage to illustrate, Lombardi makes the point that players (salespeople) hardly ever win if they don't keep trying over and over with second and third efforts.

Confidence: This is where all this leads. If we do all these things, know that we have done them, know that we are ready, then we internalize it all. Our attitudes and our confidence levels change, and we are truly armed for the Second Effort that will win.

Keeping Good People

If we don't manage, train, challenge and reward employees, we will lose them to those who will.

Keeping good people is a very real problem for all businesses. When times are tough, the grass sometimes seems particularly "greener."

I am sensitive to the issue of staff retention these days because we have just had a trio of resignations by some really fine people who were genuine contributors to our company. It's the kind of thing that sets you soul searching, looking for ways to keep it from happening in the future … wondering why it happened at all, what should be done differently.

One of those people who left our company was B.J. Eckart, the most recent publisher of *ColoradoBiz* magazine. She went for a great opportunity: president of a new division of an established company, a piece of the action and a lot of money. We really had to be happy for her even though it was hard to see her go. The other two left because the job seemed to be taking more from them than it was giving back and they wanted to be doing something else. At any rate, I was unhappy that any of them quit, much less all three. I did a little survey among some friends that asked the question, "How do you keep good people?" The consensus:

Manage well. There is plenty of discussion on just what that means, but I believe it boils down to:

- A clear job description. A person needs to know exactly what is expected of them and how they will be judged.
- They must buy in to the problems. In a very real sense, the solutions must be theirs.
- They must feel good about themselves and have a sense of accomplishment about their work.
- People need time for the rest of their lives. Few get all their satisfactions from their job. Those who perceive themselves as slaves will soon be gone.
- These things must be dealt with on an ongoing basis, almost every day. Once-a-year management (review time) does not work.

Challenge well. All agree, if good people are not challenged, they will look for a place where they will be challenged. On the other hand, an impossible project will become frustrating to the point of not being worth doing at all. We saw a lot of this around Colorado in the real estate industry. When it became impossible to sell or develop, people pulled up stakes and went elsewhere. The bottom line is that keeping good people requires a challenge that is tough but doable.

Train well. All people are boosted when they are learning. Many companies insist that training efforts go deep into the organization on a regular basis. It accomplishes many things at once. The employee is better able to do his or her job, he or she feels more important, and as a result, attitude and performance are enhanced. It is easy to forget the press of business, but the best investment we make this year might be in that of our people.

Reward well. The word "well" should be read as "smart." Money isn't everything, but it should be appropriate and enough. Most agree that a person is with the right company if they can earn a little more than they can at a similar company doing the same job, in exchange for being a little better at their job. Reward systems obviously extend beyond money. Reward with more challenge, responsibility, title, stock, words, a parking place, etc. Do it often and do it publicly and you'll find it worth the effort.

o o o

The Magic of Larry and Magic

Extraordinary team performance starts at the top.

A friend of mine was a college basketball player and played in Europe afterwards. He was a contemporary of Larry Bird and knows many basketball people up and down the ranks of the NBA. We got into a conversation the other day about what it would take to make the Denver Nuggets into a true championship contender and ended up discussing what makes a basketball team great. What my friend told me is this:

"Your No. 1 horse has to be great. Not just at the physical skill it takes but he has to inspire everybody else to play above their normal level. I have been told that, when Larry Bird was with the Celtics, he came with superior skills, worked harder on improving his skill than anyone else, was the first one to practice and the last to leave. He simply would do anything he could to help the team win. The result was that nobody wanted to let Larry down. And the level of play of everyone on the team went through the roof. And they won a lot of basketball games."

It was the same with Magic Johnson. He was that kind of hard worker, and his vision of success was adopted by the rest of the team because he believed so strongly.

So, you and I want to be the leaders of great teams in our businesses. How should we motivate ourselves? How should we measure ourselves?

Know your business. Larry and Magic were respected for their skills. Neither would have led a great team without those skills. If you want to lead the top team in your business, you have to be the expert in your business to the point that you are respected in and out of your company.

Get everybody playing. No matter how good the leader is, he/she can't do it alone. Everyone has to contribute. The true leader helps every other team member find his best self. He enables them to "take shots," come up with new ideas, take chances, etc. When the individual player sees that he/she is important to the leader, that's when they start to produce outside their former comfort zone. It's just another way of saying that you really can't get to the top without taking someone else with you. In sports or in business.

Get to know the individuals on your team. Get to know them well enough to be able to integrate their professional goals into the overall goal of the group. If somebody wants to be a better three-point shooter, help them get there! If somebody wants to be a sales manager, show 'em how!

Treat every team member as your partner. Explain the goals, explain how they will be accomplished, explain what's in it for each team member, *and then ask for buy-in.* Ask for ideas from your partners. Use ideas from your partners. You still have to be the boss, but at times it doesn't hurt to be just a partner.

Agendas! Make sure they are not always yours! If all you ever discuss is your stuff, your team will soon weaken.

Work hard! The team will work hard if the leader works hard. If the boss comes in at 10 a.m., many of the team members will not arrive until 9:45 a.m. Just let everyone know by your example that part of being good is working hard.

When everyone is playing with the confidence that they have a great plan, a great leader, and they are personally contributing to the success, that's when you get the best out of everyone. That's when work really gets to be fun.

○ ○ ○

What Makes an Exceptional Manager?

Some are good with the plan, some with people;
few are good with both.

Like a lot of companies, we have a retreat every year for our managers. We spend a day or two somewhere in the mountains, working on plans, performance and management techniques. We import a high-priced, dynamite trainer and we all get psyched. It's great! And we all hit the street for the next few months, rejuvenated and with lots of new ideas.

We do the same for our salespeople. With the same worthwhile results.

But the one thing that doesn't usually seem to change with these meetings is the relative pecking order of our managers. That is, if you were to rank everyone going into the seminar, the ranking would be the same after the seminar. All would learn and improve, of course, some more than others. But for the most part there will be no substantial change.

So, what does it take to make substantial change? How do we become better managers? What does it take to be a good manager in the first place?

There are three basic types of managers: those who are good with the plan, those who are good with people and those who are good with both.

Some managers really get into the plan. Particularly in these days of powerful spreadsheet software, a tech-minded person can organize, plan, extend, hypothesize and project until it's pretty clear what everyone must do to reach an objective. It's easy to spot this type; they have a piece of paper for every function and every person in the organization. This, of course, is all good. It enables a manager to scope and define so that the implementation of the plan will be efficient and effective and measurable.

But it takes people to implement a plan. This is the harder part. Fewer managers do a good job of the people part of the equation. To be successful at this, a manager must get things done through people. He or she must somehow make the pieces of paper called the plan become personally important to individuals who then become motivated to achieve their piece of the overall objective. The people manager somehow translates the company's financial and business goals into important personal objectives for the individual worker.

The reason that fewer managers get this done successfully is that our egos conflict with the core principle of leadership. We think that we become leaders because of some quality that others see in us when, in reality, people follow those few whom they are convinced are truly interested in their future. In World War II we did everything Roosevelt asked because we knew he was going to end the war and bring the soldiers home. In the early sixties I (along with everybody) was convinced that Kennedy would make America a better place for me.

In other words, I will give you my best work while trying my hardest to make your plan my plan, if I believe that you really want me to achieve what I see as success for myself. This is going to be hard for you because you will have to get to know me and you will have to let me know you at least enough so that I will come to trust you with my future. You will have to become genuinely interested in me, and you will have to listen in order to find out what my real goals are.

If you know a manager who is good at both, be sure to watch that person—because he or she could have a meteoric rise in your company.

Who can be an exceptional manager? Anyone who is willing to do the intellectual training necessary to improve his or her competence with the plan and at the same time willing and able to get the right people motivated to get behind the plan and make it happen.

○ ○ ○

Outlasting Hard Times

Before long, we won't have to be thinking like this.

If your business is anything like ours at Wiesner Publishing, your whole organization gets a lot of energy and enthusiasm from the sales team. They come back with war stories of how they finally edged out the competition and tall tales of how our product won the day! Their feelings of accomplishment and success are shared by all. It's one of our connections with the real world, our customer. It is an important measure of our effectiveness as a company.

So what happens when times are tough? What happens when the victories are farther apart? Right now, most would agree that many Colorado companies (us included) are dealing with hard times. With this in mind, we asked some known "copers" and survivors what they think are the keys to enduring our present situation so that we will be able to enjoy the growth we all know is coming to Colorado. The answers fall into these three categories:

Financial planning. Be conservative. Plan for the hard times you're in. Don't let wishful thinking cause you to schedule a recovery before it is really ready to happen. Make sure that your conservative business plan allows you to make it in the worst-case scenario, well beyond the expected upturn. Show this plan to your accountant and work together on it until you both agree it's doable and reasonable.

Work your plan. Pay attention to your plan: Cut the cloth to fit the suit! Work harder and smarter than you ever have. Don't put up with anyone on your team who is not pulling more than his or her fair share. Replace them if they are not; it is your responsibility to the business and the others who depend on it. Stick to the budget. Make sacrifices. Make sure you perform for your customers; they are all trying to maximize results too.

Attitude. A key part of keeping it together in hard times: Each manager worth his or her salt must be the Keeper of Attitudes for everyone in the company they come in contact with. Some things the better manager will do: Spend more time as a "cheerleader" than you think is necessary. Because there should be a reward for hard work even when the results are thin because of the economy, find ways to bestow accolades, distinction and honor. Money probably is not appropriate or available, and the long-haul employee will know it.

Small successes are still successes and should be shared with the entire company. Everyone is part of the fabric of the company spirit. Don't expect what just can't be delivered. If the level of available business is down, it should be reflected in your plan, because if you try to beat it out of your sales department, you will ruin good people. Don't let your salespeople burn out. Help them do something different—take a day off, go to the zoo with the kids, etc. Loss of perspective when things are difficult can lead to general despair, and you could be shipping another good employee to California.

Good luck!

o o o

The Most Important Right of All

We in America don't realize just how important a free press is.
Without it, none of our other rights are real.

I was sitting in the lobby bar of the Crillon Hotel in Lima, Peru. This was the main American hotel in town. Just about everyone spoke at least a little English, enough to help you get by.

I had just come from a walk of a dozen or so blocks up the street to the Plaza, the center of town, and back. I couldn't believe the chaos, the tension, the pending violence and the military presence on the streets. There were tanks everywhere. Soldiers patrolled in twos with what looked like machine guns at the ready. An open truckload of 20 or more noisy, shouting men in red caps, brandishing sticks or bats, careened around a comer and sped down a side street and disappeared around a second corner. I was shaken and not just a little frightened as I came in from the street to sit in this very American-looking lobby bar.

The most unforgettable part was that the news on the TV over the bar mentioned none of it. Nor did the newspaper. They covered everything else, from international tensions to the local soccer problems, but never mentioned the problems in the streets.

I asked the bartender, "Why?"

He told me simply that the government controlled the TV and the paper. He did not elaborate. He thought it should be obvious.

That was 12 years ago. Nothing has changed, and things are worse in Peru, I'm told.

I recently visited Dachau in Germany. The people of this lovely little Bavarian town bravely keep a museum there, to remind the world that the atrocities of the Nazi death camps must never happen again. As I went through the museum and walked the grounds it seemed a bit clearer to me how a few madmen could make this happen in the midst of a country full of decent people. There was no way for a national conscience to form. Hitler had burned all the books and taken over all the radio stations and newspapers. In addition to all the other troubles of the times, there was no way to know what your neighbors were thinking. No free press. No free speech. No way for opinion to accumulate.

Recent events in the Soviet Union provide a strikingly positive example of the power of the free press. Even though the communists tried to close down the free flow of information, they could not. The people had some three years of a relatively free press and would not give it up. Photocopied street newspapers told the truth. People gathered. People spoke. The state of communications in today's world is such that the Muscovites knew that every country in the world was with them (except Cuba and Iraq)! Opinion accumulated and multiplied, and the people would not be denied.

I sometimes find myself criticizing the local newspapers and TV stations for being inaccurate or doing an unwarranted hatchet job or twisting the news for entertainment reasons or because they seem to be constantly negative on Denver. But if they and every other paper and broadcast outlet in the U.S. didn't have the right to say whatever they believed to be correct, we would have the same problems as Peru or China or Cuba. The rest of the Bill of Rights would be meaningless.

What "Tough" Means in Selling

If you filled Mile High Stadium with 76,000 businesspeople of all sorts, there would only be 50 really top sales producers among them. It would be tough to find them in the crowd.

Selling is a hard job. One in 10 tries it. One in 50 sticks with it for at least two years. One in 400 makes a career of it, and one in 1,600 makes it to the top 25 percent, who are the best-paid, best-respected salespeople in business.

Selling is a hard job. How do you know that you have what it takes to be successful? Here are some simple characteristics that we find in the best salespeople who work for us:

The best can take a punch and seem to turn it into positive energy. Many people just can't take the negative stuff, the rejection that everybody in sales gets, and that's why they quit sales. The good ones seem to be unfazed by the rejection. I remember once when John Ralston, a Denver Broncos coach of days gone by, told me that good football players really liked getting hit. To them it is more of an energizer than an energy-sapper. It's like that with a good salesman after a bad call.

The best are really hard to say no to. If the prize is worthwhile, the really good salespeople keep on coming. They're usually also smart; they realize that once someone says "no," it is usually fruitless to just keep pounding. Instead, they get more ammo. We have a great young salesman on the phone for us now who, when he gets a genuine "no," is off the phone just long enough to get new information for a new approach. He gets lots of job offers just based on his persistence.

The best do the hard stuff first. Always make the hardest call first. Try the biggest possibility first. Take the biggest risk for the biggest payoff. While at it, top salespeople ask the toughest questions first and don't easily let the client get off with anything less than a full answer. The best salespeople always ask the question that is on their mind, whatever it is.

The best command respect. If you have a salesperson sounding like a doormat, don't look for big things. Ever hear a sales type say something like:

"Oh thank you so much *(because I don't deserve it)* for taking time out of your busy schedule *(you are much more important than me)* to see me. I'll be very brief *(because what I have to say isn't very important!)*"? Not the good ones. The best know they are there to provide needed help to their clients, and so they will take the time they need.

The best don't internalize turn-downs. Good sales types realize that the best way to get your mind off a bad result or bad call is to do another one, right away! This is easy to say, and sales management everywhere preaches it, but when you see someone doing it, you have a "more ammo!" winner.

The best balance two competing sales pressures. Good salespeople want to sell as much as they can to whomever can afford to buy, and they will never sell anything to anyone who doesn't need or can't use the product or service.

No one can guarantee success, but some people work so smart they certainly deserve it.

○ ○ ○

My Last Column

This is a preview.

Somebody asked me what I would write about if this were my last column. This is what it might be.

I will want to make the point that despite the likes of Eliot Spitzer, Bill Clinton, Joe Nacchio and Ken Lay, the world is full of people who are worth knowing, even worth emulating. Great partners and great customers alike abound. To find them you've just got to look for them and relate to them.

My business partner and I were having lunch in a fine restaurant along a beautiful beach in La Ceiba, Honduras. Along came a mutual business friend with his two kids—two lovely young girls, one about age 5 and the other about 8. We exchanged warm greetings with our friend, and then he said to his daughters, "Girls, these are my good friends from the U.S." These beautiful young ladies came over and gave me a hug, and the older of the two even gave me a peck on the cheek.

I was shocked because in this country people don't teach their kids to do stuff like this anymore. Actually, our kids are taught to shy away from strangers, to not trust anyone. Who knows what evil lurks ...

Conditioned by TV news coverage, we teach our kids that most of the world we live in is very dangerous. The news is 95 percent crime, mayhem, murder, infidelity. Lying, cheating, whoring, stealing—it seems sometimes that everyone is just out for themselves. But the real truth I'd argue is that your TV doesn't portray nearly a real or fair view of the world.

I would try to write something to young people, kids in college or high school. I would try to say something about the incredible build-up in the newspapers, magazines and TV of evidence supporting the idea that there can't be an honest politician or businessman anywhere on Earth. If all you did was read the paper and watch TV, you would think there were no faithful husbands (or wives), no politicians who don't steal, no businesses that aren't trying to shortchange the customer and take millions for themselves, and no priests who aren't predators.

But it is not true. I think it sells papers, and people just like to read about it. I have been in the business world about 50 years. I've been a salesman, writer, manager and owner. I have been party to a hundred deals, and I've been involved in selling and buying many millions of dollars of magazines.

I can't think of anyone in my history who was truly corrupt. Perhaps there were a couple of people we decided to stay away from, but in life everyone has to do that once in a while.

The point is that the world is full of worthwhile people. Go find a few and do great things.

Of course, there is dishonesty in the world. I overheard some businessmen in an airport discussing corruption in our country and abroad among government employees, but they don't represent the majority.

The world is full of good honest people anxious to find the same kind of people to be around, to build a world with.

If I could write about one idea and make it stick, I would tell young people, "Study hard; don't pay any attention to the bad guys; take the high road; have fun and make something good happen."

I'll start thinking about it now so that when the time comes for my last column, I'll have it all figured out.

Graduation Wisdom

Good ideas for management come from everywhere. These are from high school graduation speeches.

I recently attended a couple of high school graduation ceremonies. I don't know why I wasn't expecting it, but I was surprised that the speakers, young and old alike, gave thoughtful and helpful advice.

It seems good advice is good for everybody, whether an 18-year-old just starting out or a proven manager trying to get the best work from his team. Here are some thoughts that stuck with me:

Be incredibly curious about the world around you. At all ages, the more competent we believe ourselves to be, the more we tend to talk than to listen. The truly capable people are always listening, asking questions and learning from others. They're not trying to selfishly suck information from others; rather, they really care about the people they meet.

A manager like this is better equipped to make decisions because he/she not only knows a lot about business but also about people, their goals and aspirations and what is likely to motivate them.

Happiness comes 90 percent from who you are and 10 percent from what you have. We all know negative examples of those with money: the unhappy miser, the rudderless trust-funder, etc. The distinction is less clear but no less true when talking about those with power.

In college, I knew pre-med students who would not share the time of day, much less ideas on a homework assignment, with other pre-med students. They were uptight, hungry for the power of class and position, and everyone was the enemy.

Similarly, there are managers more interested in their own success and accumulating power than in anything or anyone else. They might be managers, but they aren't leaders.

There are happy people who have money and things and those who don't. Have you met a happy person, rich or not so rich, who thought money or power had much to do with his/her happiness? Isn't happiness usually measured in our opinion of how we are doing with our relationships?

I'm not sure where you're going, but I want to go with you. True friendship, true love, true leadership, each on its own level. It's a level of commitment seldom received. It can come from a best friend, a spouse, perhaps. It happens rarely in a lifetime.

In business, it is something of a mystery when we get good people to throw in with us to pursue what is mostly our goal. Sometimes it's the power of an idea, other times of a personality.

When a leader gets this kind of commitment, great things can be accomplished. To continue to deserve this high level of trust, it must be returned. Those giving it must feel the recipients want to go with them as well. It is the essence of a team.

In the final analysis, wisdom and compassion are the same. This insight was suggested by Ralph Taylor, an English teacher at Aurora's Regis High. What better advice could be given to young people going out to seek fortune and fame? Or to CEOs of Fortune 500 companies?

If you would be wise, then care honestly about all those in your life, at home, in the office and in your community.

Good advice to the graduating class? You bet. And if we want to be better managers, leaders, spouses, parents or whatever, we should listen carefully, too.

Believe in Me

The motivational force from which all others are derived.

A young man I know finally got his first job a couple of months ago. He graduated from college two years ago, and spent the following year wandering around Spain enjoying himself, and not earning much more than a pretty good facility with the Spanish language. He finally ran out of money and prospects because, just like in the United States, in Spain it's difficult for a foreigner to get a visa that allows one to get a job.

So in the middle of last year he returned to the U.S. thinking seriously about starting a career.

He liked the idea of a job in sales. He was good with people and figured that sales was a pretty good way to the top if he was good at it. He could only dream of someday getting into something where he could use his fondness for the Spanish language.

The problem seemed to be the economy. Times were bad, and nobody was hiring anyone, much less a green college grad with a liberal arts education and a year in Spain under his belt. There followed dozens of interviews and tests that generated an equal number of discouraging results.

Finally, he was offered a job as an inside salesman in a division of a large company. He wasn't really sure it was what he wanted because he saw himself as an outside salesman, dealing face-to-face with his customers and prospects. But it made sense to start someplace and begin to build experience.

He was surprised and delighted to discover that he had been hired because of his knowledge of Spanish, and the company made him the inside customer service rep for Mexico! He felt on top of the world working every day on the phone with Mexican buyers.

And it got even better.

A few weeks ago, the outside salesman took this young man on a two-week trip to Mexico to meet a number of potential customers. They set sales records! In less than two weeks, they sold hundreds of thousands of dollars of new business in a new market, far away and culturally much different from their own!

What happened here?

I had the chance to ask the young man why he thought they did so well. "Those Mexican companies could have bought our kind of product from lots of Americans," he told me.

"But they weren't looking for technical superiority, they were looking for an American supplier who *believed in Mexico*. Because we came to them and both of us tried to speak their language and we were genuinely excited about their project, they decided that we were that American supplier."

First, it's impressive that a 23-year-old could pick up on the idea that there is no stronger motivator than "I believe in you!" He has great prospects for success. More important is the concept.

As managers we will have incredible team success if team members know that we *believe in them*. As parents, our children will have a great jump on life if they start with the knowledge that *we believe in them*. We help our friends immeasurably by giving them good reason to know that *we believe in them*.

It can't be phony. If we try to trick someone by pretending, he will pick up on it, and we will seem insincere. But if I am convinced that you truly believe in me, I will give you my best work, my complete loyalty, and I will work very hard to make you successful.

This is the first and most fundamental law of motivation.

Successful, or Significant?

The question can be put to just about any human endeavor.

"Mr. Big, you have accomplished a lot in your life and with your business. No question, you are financially successful. But ask yourself: Are you financially significant? Would you like to be financially significant? What would that mean to you?"

I was having lunch with a young man, Brett Derosier, because we have a common interest in airplanes. Our conversation wandered, as these things often do, to each of our businesses. His has to do with helping high-net-worth individuals manage their particular minefields. He told me that the above concept was one that often motivated such people to do great things—build hospitals and universities, create scholarships, fund museums, etc.

One can be financially successful without being financially significant. The only way to be significant is to give something back, to help someone else be better off than they would have been.

Not very many of us will struggle with turning our financial success into significance. But we can certainly apply this idea to other areas in which we would like to be "significant."

Management: A successful manager is one who runs a group that makes its numbers, is efficient, has below-average turnover, is accurately budgeted, has a good grasp of the future and has a plan for it.

A significant manager does all this but also gets the best possible work out of the people in his/her charge by leading them to become their best selves. This can only be accomplished by taking the time to find out the individual goals and aspirations of each member of the team and framing their job so that they can realize their goals along with those of the company. Those being managed get as much or more than the company.

A significant manager also will create a model for management excellence that lasts for years to come in the company.

Sales: In addition to those things you'd expect from a successful salesperson—numbers, calls, plans, hard work—the significant salesperson will truly help his/her customers solve their problems; it will seem to customers that they have at last found a salesperson who does more than ask for more business. The significant salesperson will build customer relations that will accrue to the company and outlast the salesperson in that job. This territory will be a snap for the next guy as our significant salesperson moves up in the company.

Friend: Consider the difference between a friend and a significant friend. A significant friend will be someone who we will never forget because he or she will have made some positive contribution to our life or our success that was beyond the bounds of a normal acquaintanceship or friendship. (I had a friend who pushed me really hard as a young man. He made me get good at selling. There wasn't much in it for him other than the good feeling that comes from helping someone else. He, to me, was a significant friend.)

To be considered "significant" at anything, from financial to boss to father-in-law, we must do something beyond the ordinary "successful" and make a contribution to the people around us. We have to give back without getting.

Management Vision

Some have it and some don't. We are fortunate if we work for someone who has it.

I ran into Ted the other day. I hadn't seen him in years; I learned a lot from him when we worked together. Ted and Sid were friends of mine. They had joined the company within one month of each other, and we worked together as advertising space salesmen.

Then both were promoted to sales manager positions on different magazines. Both had had stellar careers as field salesmen, earned a shot at management and were excited to move up. Both had been company leaders as salesmen, were known as hard workers and renowned for their people skills. Both were slated for big things with the company. Everyone knew they would succeed. But only one did. In 10 years, Sid rose to the top. He spent the last half of his career as one of a handful of people in the inner sanctum in a $400 million company. He was fulfilled and successful. Ted lasted about 1 1/2 years in sales management before he returned to being a salesman on the advice of what today would be called the human resources manager.

Years later, I asked the HR guy why he thought one of these seemingly equal candidates made it big and the other didn't. He told me Sid had a global view of the company and his job that Ted never figured out. He told me Sid was like a good NFL quarterback in that he could see nearly the whole field at one time and simultaneously keep track of all the dynamics.

Sid rose quickly and took a lot of good people with him. The HR guy also said Ted always seemed to be looking at his job through a cardboard roller from the center of a toilet paper roll. He could see only one small spot of his world at a time. While he was occupied with it, the other parameters wandered so much, he could never catch up with everything at the same time. Ted dealt with everyone on his team as though there were only two on the team, himself and the person he was working with at the moment.

I used to analyze these two, looking for clues to success. For some reason, it all seems clearer now:

A successful manager takes the time to know the problems of all team members. We really can't do this from the comfort of our own offices. We must go out on the floor, talk to people and find out what is going on. We need to listen and then put everything into perspective.

A successful manager solves team member problems through other team members. There's no better way to help others grow and learn some of the real secrets of management, i.e., our biggest strengths are found in the undiscovered abilities of those around us.

A successful manager realizes the real challenge of management is to get good work out of ordinary people by helping them see themselves in light of what they dream of becoming.

This is why people who make it to the top always seem to take a lot of good people with them. They seem to have an extra share of luck because they are surrounded by happy, productive people.

Sweet Land of Liberty

Freedom is what makes this country unique. Let's be very careful
before we give up any of it for more security.

At times like these one wonders if somehow we aren't, inch by inch,
cutting away at the fabric of the country that once was. Is it true that
it used to be a lot better than it is now? Can we survive the thinking that
causes any citizen to take action that results in the World Trade Center and
Oklahoma City disasters? Will we ever stop arguing among ourselves about
affirmative action, term limits and *the size of government*? Is racism eating away
at our ability to be one country? Are we exporting our children's jobs? Is
our civilization using drugs and alcohol to numb itself to the reality of our
situation? Can we stop shooting each other at random or even by accident?

Is Bill or Newt or anybody smart enough to replace the Welfare State
with a state of hope, jobs and prosperity? Is America fair? Can only the
very selfish and the very aggressive get ahead? Does business really want to
rape the workers so that it can pay millions per year to a few owners and
managers? Are labor unions just a bunch of mobsters out to line their own
pockets? Will we have any security at all in our old age? Will our kids ever
respect their parents? Are things just getting worse?

Is the American Dream still alive? You bet! Why? Because we are free. Liberty.
The very characteristic that forces us to live with a few Timothy McVeigh's
gives promise to our children and their children that the United States can be
a better place for them. We have the tools to solve problems.

One time last year the Immigration and Naturalization Service came to a
local hotel and collected all the undocumented Mexicans and exported them
by plane back to Mexico. This took place on Thursday. By Monday more than
half were back in Denver reporting for work. These people didn't come back
because of welfare, they came back to work. They know that in America,
despite all our problems, you can improve your lot. You can work hard and
achieve; you can educate yourself for a better life and you can realistically
expect the next generation will achieve even more.

I recently interviewed a visiting Russian journalist and asked what he
thought was the biggest difference between America and his country. He

shrugged and laughed a little as though the answer should be so obvious that it was almost a silly question. "You have had freedom for 200 years and we have been free for only two," he said, nodding vigorously, "and freedom gives everybody a better chance for a better life."

In a conversation a couple years ago, a nightclub singer from South America told me, "You Americans don't realize that what you have is very special. It is what makes all the Mexicans and Cubans and Haitians try to get into your country ... a chance, an opportunity to make your own way. Yours is one of the few countries in the world where people can work their way up in society."

To the extent that we are free, we can solve all our problems. Free to come and go, to assemble, to speak our minds, to vote, to live in peace and, yes, to bear arms. To give up even little pieces of any of these rights for any reason is to start down a road that will suck the energy and life out of this country.

We often ask ourselves what kind of country we are handing our children and grandchildren. In some ways, we may be giving them our problems that we inherited from parents, but if we give them less freedom, we will be taking the only tools known to man to work in solving these problems. We would be taking away the exact stuff that makes having them worthwhile.

Sometimes We Don't Get It Right When We Try to Motivate People

Money is No. 8!

The last two years of high school and all through college, I worked in home construction in the town where I grew up. A friend of mine had a job as a carpenter's assistant and helped me get a job as a laborer. The first year I carried lumber, the second they gave me a hammer and nails, and I learned to be a pretty good hand and earned a lot more per hour than most of the other kids my age.

We worked for a builder named Fred Ingalls. Fred had a way of making work fun. For example, he would typically come to the job site after lunch, when my buddy and I were doing something like putting siding on a new house. Fred would start talking about some guys who used to work for him who were really good at siding, and the conversation would end with something like, "I'll bet that you guys can't finish the front of this house by 4 o'clock!" We would declare loudly that we were the best siding putter-on-ers he ever saw. We would take the bet. The stakes? A milkshake!

So, two young kids, working by the hour, would proceed to do a day's work in two hours for a milkshake, because the milkshake came with lots of recognition and approval. We knew that Fred believed we were very good at our jobs, and that he would brag about us around the construction community. It was worth it.

Not long ago, I heard a presentation by Kraig Kramers, a management consultant, about a study that showed that when it comes to motivators, money was ranked eighth! So, what were one and two? Recognition and growth potential.

We live in a world that seems to regard money over everything else. "Show me the money!" easily leaps off the silver screen into our management mode of operation. We often make the mistake of thinking that money is everything. It's not. It's not even close; it's eighth. We won't get much done without money, but it is so much better if it comes wrapped with other things.

Some thoughts about recognition: As Kramers says, set up recognition systems to catch people doing things right. Then reward and recognize. It's a lot better if everybody knows about it. Celebrate success and recognition throughout the organization.

It should be deserved and everyone should agree. Recognition that is really flattery will undermine your credibility for a long time.

It should happen often. Annual recognition is great, but monthly is better. Best is being aware and giving recognition when it's deserved, particularly in those areas of your company/department that are often overlooked.

Some thoughts about growth potential: Growth from within is preferred. People who we develop from our organizations have the culture, and we know them well. Promotions from within make everyone in the organization feel good about the company.

We are all unsure of our strengths and our potential. A good boss helps every person in his/her department not only see their potential but achieve it.

A good leader helps people see themselves in light of their strengths, even though they might be unaware or unsure of some of these strengths.

Nobody will ever be aware of their growth potential if we don't communicate well. Help your people, particularly the real winners, see their potential and then help them plan to achieve it.

As Kramers says, "Remember, communication only works if it is repetitive."

Remember, communication only works if it is repetitive.

Judge Not ...

The truth in business and in life: We're judged all the time.

You walk into a room full of people you have never met before to have a meeting about something you are all concerned about. It could be a business meeting or a session of your homeowners' association. Suppose it lasts an hour or so. By the time everyone has had their say you will have made some judgments about each of the people in the room. You will have established some sort of pecking order about each of the participants in the discussion, measured your regard for them, and determined a value for what each has to say.

So will everyone else in the room. Each person will make a ranking of everyone else. Who is the strongest? Who is the weakest? Who would I like to have on my team? Who would I work for? A lot of this may not be conscious, but, if not, it still occurs just below the surface.

I have been a salesman almost my whole life. I figure that my average customer has at least 25 salespeople just like me calling on them. And I know that my customer has a ranking in his head for each of us. It might not be something he thinks about every day, but he could easily tell you which sales people he hopes never call him again, and which ones he is happy to hear back from.

So if I'm an average salesman, I'll be in the middle of the pack of that bunch of 25, and I'll probably have a hard time getting to see Mr. Big. I'll be average in my sales performance, and I'll make an average income and probably have an average life. I probably have learned to do things like most other salespeople do them.

If, on the other hand, I am not like the other 24 if I dress differently, act differently, perform better, provide more information to the customer, sound less like I'm only interested in myself and my product, contribute to the solution of my customer's problems, etc., then things will be different for me.

I will move up in the rankings that my customer is sure to make of his list of 25. I will find it easier to get appointments (because I always bring value, net just my product). I will make more money than my peers, and I will possibly be happier for it.

So the question for me becomes: "How can I move up in the pecking order that my customer has for all the salespeople calling on him?" I believe it comes down to a single principle. Bring a lot more to the table than your product.

How many times have you heard a sales rep (or heard yourself) say something like, "My name is Fred and I'm with XYZ, and I'd like to stop by and drop off my card and ask you a few questions about your plans to buy our type of product to see if perhaps we might be able to help you."

What kind of ranking do you score among all the calls Mr. Big will get today? You will be able to make a living doing that, but you will be in the middle of the pack at best.

If we could say something like, "I have new information about your share of the market. Would you like to see it?" we would do much better with the customer. If we delivered on our claim, we would surely move up on his list of preferred callers.

But to deliver on the claim also takes a lot of research and work. The top guys get it done! To be successful in any arena of business sales, management, production, etc., it helps to be aware that everyone we deal with has a list, a pecking order. To move up that list we have to produce for that person. Help solve their problems first.

o o o

Manager or Leader

Which do you want to be?

"She never really bosses me around or gets in the way of me doing my job, but she has the knack of knowing a lot about what I'm doing and of being able to help when I need it."

This was the response to my "Why?" when I was told by an acquaintance recently that he really liked working for his boss.

"What else makes her a good boss?" I asked.

"I know she likes me; she gives me a lot of positive feedback while at the same time I know that she always will tell me what she really is thinking. And I'm sure that she cares about my future. I'm not just a cog in the wheel who will help her achieve her goals. I'd like to help her because I know if she wins then I'll win."

A manager is one who marshals resources, organizes forces, directs strategies and uses information to control and redirect all of these eventually to accomplish well-thought-out goals and objectives. You can manage time, or machines, or money and even people without being a leader.

You can put the right combination of people with the right talents on the right problem with the right machinery and even get the job done right without being a leader ... if you're a good manager.

But only a leader gets the best work out of people and helps them grow to be the people they dream of becoming. At least if you will agree that the principal business definition of a leader is someone who can get workers and employees to contribute their very best work to the company, to work in a way that fulfills them and helps them grow as well as enables them to enjoy contributing their best work.

Further questions of the person in the conversation above, and others who seem fortunate to work for bosses (read: leaders) who bring out the best in them, reveal the following characteristics of leaders:

A leader knows what is happening everywhere in his or her operating theater. They do this by spending a lot of time with everyone who reports to them. Time asking questions about what is going on. Not in a challenging way but a way that supports, reinforces, informs, instructs and gives the leader-manager a real sense of what really is going on.

For example, a sales manager who also is a leader will periodically sit with every salesman in his charge and go through his or her entire account list, asking, suggesting, reinforcing and learning. A production manager who is a leader regularly will ask each of his employees about problems, suggestions, solutions. A manager will try to do it from reports.

A leader will convince each person entrusted to him or her that the individual's future is important and part of the overall plan for the group's success, that the group cannot succeed unless the individual also succeeds. If the "leader" doesn't believe this about every individual in his group, those in the group are wrong for this leader, or ... the leader really isn't one. The leader will take the time to find out what each individual considers his or her individual success. The manager will be focused on team performance.

A leader does not do everything, but he or she knows everything that is being done. There is a sort of code of "no surprises" between a leader and his or her people. It works both ways, or it doesn't work at all. The manager will be more of a loner.

A leader encourages while correcting, but he or she corrects. None of a leader's relationships is contrived; they all are built on honesty. The role of a leader in modern management is becoming more important. If we begin to think of ourselves as leaders as well as managers, our companies will prosper and our people will be happier.

Which are you? Which do you really want to be?

o o o

Everybody Pick Up a Rock!

Leadership and management in early times were about
the same as now

You just can't believe it what they built in Europe in the 1600s and even earlier. My wife and I recently took what we think of as a dream trip, spending a couple of weeks in Spain and Portugal. Lots of jokes are made about all the castles and palaces, but they are everywhere and they are incredible.

This country, the U.S., is just 200 years old. Portugal and Spain are 2,200 years old! We are just beginners. If you want to see something older than 200 years in this country you have to start looking at mountains or other geography.

In Portugal you leave an "Autopista" as good as any part of Interstate 25 in Colorado, and instantly take a 600-year trip back in time. The streets in the towns become one-car wide and are made of cobblestone, and just about every burg is complete with a castle built on top of the biggest hill and often surrounded by what is left of a protective city wall built by Moors or Romans.

We saw the ruins of Roman aqueducts and houses built some 200 years B.C. At times I felt like James Bond driving through narrow streets between the old buildings with people needing to jump out of the way as I passed.

While we were visiting a beautiful, huge castle, the exterior at least twice the size of Denver's sports arena, I wondered out loud how they could have done this without tools, cranes, trucks, bulldozers, etc. One of the caretakers told us it took 50,000 men some 30 years to build it. This is more people than work for United Airlines! How did they do it? How did they get anything done? Very few could read or write; there was no way to talk to 100 men at a time, much less 50,000.

The problems of leadership and management had to be massive. First, you have to get everyone willing and ready to pick up a rock. Probably in those days slavery was a pretty strong motivator. But the results were so beautiful and have lasted so long that I can't believe that a lot of it wasn't done with lots of care and pride. That would have required some real, people-oriented leadership.

After you have 50,000 men eager to get the work done, someone has to manage them. This must have taken incredible skills in planning and organizing, directing, getting feedback and then directing changes. Laborers, rock cutters, masons, carpenters, architects and on and on ... had to be inspired and organized.

The often-blurred relationship between "leadership" and "management" becomes pretty clear in this case; it takes a leader to get thousands of men to want to haul building materials up the mountain and to do a good job of assembling the materials, and it takes a great manager to plan and organize the workers to get the job done.

Perhaps it can give us some clues as to how to run our own businesses.

We have to be a leader to get people to charge the problem. This can only be done if the people doing the charging see their work as somehow worthy, a way to achieve their own goals. It's up to the leader to relate the results of the effort to the goals and aspirations of the doers. Obviously; the leader has to find out what that connection might be.

The manager then has to have a plan that inspires success, the organizational skills to efficiently keep all the parts synchronized, and a feedback system that allows smooth control and communication.

If we measure ourselves by both sets of criteria, perhaps we can become good enough to be considered both a leader and a manager.

○ ○ ○

Micromanagement Kills

Micromanaging erases leadership points you may have had, limits your promotion prospects and makes you a lousy coach or teacher. Otherwise, it sometimes gets the job done.

If you want to see how to destroy someone with micromanagement, just stop at some soccer field in your area where young kids are playing. You are bound to find a parent somewhere micromanaging his or her kid. You've seen it before. It goes something like this:

"Run to the ball, Billy! Faster! No, not that side, the other side! No, the other way! Kick it with the other foot! Harder! No, not to him! To him! Back up! No, the other side! Get it! Get it! The other foot! Harder! Now turn!"

(The kid, for some strange reason, falls down.)

"Don't fall down! Get up! Run!"

And so forth.

When someone is learning something, obviously he can't think about the process as fast as someone who already has the skill. So it is easy for the teacher (manager) to one-up the learner at every step because the learner has to pause at each step and think through the process. It's like when you study a new language. At first you have to translate each word before going to the next. When you start to get good at a language, you skip the translating part and just use words for their meaning.

When a kid is trying to learn something new or an employee is trying to think through a new idea that has been presented and the manager (parent) will not let him have the time to take even one step on his own, bad things happen. The person being badly managed loses interest, resents the manager and never gets good at soccer or selling or whatever.

I was once trying to learn to operate a boat that was bigger than anything I had run before. This was a serious machine with two big diesel engines. A captain helped me as I learned to go from A to B and how to get into and out of slips at crowded marinas. The basic problem was that I never thought I could catch up to what he was telling me. He would say something like, "Come left!" and before I could process the command, understand why it made sense, and then move my hands on the helm, he would say, "Come left!!!" I could never please him because I wasn't fast enough.

It made me mad, made me feel stupid and sort of wrecked the experience.

I found that the only way I could begin to please him was to do what I was told without thinking, without any input from me. I was only trying to do the mechanical things he told me ("port reverse!" or "starboard forward!"). I didn't learn very much, and I lost a lot of the confidence I had started with.

It's been said here many times: To become more valuable to your company, become a builder of people. A micromanager not only doesn't build anybody, he/she ruins people—makes them confused and angry, and turns them into poor employees who quit to go find another company that is better to work for.

If you have a boss who has all the ideas, if he/she does all the talking in your meetings, if the others in your group hesitate before making suggestions, if everyone just carries out orders, if each and every small step is scrutinized, he/she is probably a micromanager. The fix for this management malfunction is easy to say but hard to do, like a lot of things.

The micromanager should start by picking just one person in his or her life, and make it a No. 1 priority to help him/her grow to be the kind of person he/she wants to be. That person will learn what success is all about and how good it feels.

When finished with the first, the micromanager should pick another. In the process, the micromanager will drop his "micro" and become one of the most valuable managers in his company.

o o o

More on Keeping Good People

Management's greatest task: Inspiring and nurturing the people who will make the company—and you—successful.

Earlier this month I found myself on a panel at a trade show on "How to Keep Good People." Our goal soon focused on coming up with a list of things that every manager present could take back to their own businesses and put to work. We started with the idea of "20 steps I can take to keep good people." Before we were finished our list had grown to more than 50. I'd like to pass along as many as I can in this space.

The meeting started with a lot of discussion trying for some sort of definition of the environment that attracts and keeps good people. This is it stated from the point of view of the person managed: "If I know that you are *genuinely* and *actively* concerned about my success, then I will give you my best, most enthusiastic work, because I know that if you succeed, so will I."

Obviously, this is one of those easy-to-say, hard-to-do statements. We agreed that one must pay careful attention to the words highlighted. For example, *genuinely* and *actively* means that your interest cannot be pasted on and you must do more than listen; you must act. In order to be concerned about my success, you must know how I define success for myself.

With this as a starting point, we began developing a list of concrete action items. Again, written from the point of view of the person being managed and in no particular order:

Listen. Not just once during a yearly review, but regularly to find out my goals and frustrations.

Be consistent and fair. If you want a lot of turnover, be the kind of boss that no one can figure out.

Give energy. Some managers seem to take something from you every time you deal with them. Be the kind of boss that gives support enthusiasm, credit, encouragement.

Use my talents and abilities. If you do, you will be a boss in a million and I will give you my best effort.

Expect a high level of performance. Tell me exactly what it will take for you to say, "Job well done!"

Trust me. Treat me like I'm important and like I know what I am doing. You will be pleased with the result far more often than you will be disappointed.

Tell me often what I am doing right and why you are glad I work for you.

Talk about those things that you don't think I'm doing as well as I should. Again, not just once a year during a review, but regularly so that the air will always be clear.

Ask me what I think. Then listen. If you value what I say, I will value what you say.

Get rid of negative people. If someone does not fit, it is the manager's job to help them find another place to work.

Have a sense of humor. People do their best work when they are having fun doing it.

Reward performance. Remember that money may mean little without opportunity or recognition. You must know how I define success for myself.

Treat people like people, not employees. For this you will get back honesty.

You can probably continue making a list for as long as you care to think about it, just like we did. When I returned to Denver I asked my 11-year-old his opinion, just for the heck of it, and he told me: "Don't be too strict and learn everybody's name."

I would say that deep down we all know how to keep good people, but when we become managers we sometimes forget.

Six Traits That Make a "One-in-5O" Salesperson

If you come across someone who is pleasant and fits this description, you probably are dealing with a very successful salesperson.

We all have to put up with salespeople in our lives, whether we are in sales ourselves or not.

My guess would be somewhere around 20 to 30 a day, ranging from the guy at Krispy Kreme in the morning trying to sell you an extra dozen, to the stock salesman who calls in the middle of the day to trick you into buying his pick, to the lady who calls you at home during dinner to read you her pitch. And lots more!

Most aren't very good at their job, and we (and I suspect they) know it.

The problem all of us salespeople have is to stand out and be the "one in 50" that is really good, one who people like to hear from and like to be around. What does it take, and how can we measure it?

A great salesperson is a great listener. People who think they want to try sales often say, "I like people and I get along well with them. I think I'd do really well in sales." Often this turns out to be code for "I like to talk, I like to tell." Two tendencies not found in good salespeople.

Recently one of our managers described one of our most successful salespeople as a "world class listener." In my book, the highest accolade. Those talkers with the "gift of gab" might make a living, but they will be working for the true listeners.

A great salesperson is a skillful questioner. You'll know you're in the presence of a successful salesperson when you find yourself answering questions about yourself and your business that you probably had no intention of discussing. And more or less enjoying it. We sense that this person is not just trying to push product but is interested in understanding the problem.

A great salesperson brings more to the table than his or her product. The great majority of sales folk make themselves average or less by talking intelligently about only one thing, their product. All they seem to be able to do is tell how great their widget is and ask for the order.

A great salesperson is tough. Toughness in selling has a couple of components. First is simply the ability to take rejection and keep punching. Particularly if we are "people pleasing" salespeople, everyone senses that we are easy to say "no" to, and many even make a game of it.

It's a tough business and takes backbone. The good ones love the competitive nature of it. Rejection merely makes them more intent on getting the business by coming up with a better solution to the customer's problem.

A great salesperson has an objective. He or she has a goal for a sales call and won't quit before reaching it. The same is true about his or her career and family. The really good salesperson doesn't let one of these suffer on account of the other.

A great salesperson possesses two critical characteristics in equal measure. He or she does not like to lose for any reason. Yet he or she would never sell anyone something they can't use or don't need. These two seem to conflict at times, but the great salesperson considers both precepts as inviolable.

o o o

Take Someone with You to the Top

Lots of us want success, but many of us think getting there is a solitary effort.

It was a dinner for college scholarship award winners at Metro State College of Denver. A man of some 30-plus years, one of the honorees, David Merrill, stood at the microphone telling us his story. He was now finally finishing up his degree after giving college a second try.

When he was much younger, his first attempt ended with him dropping out. After a few years in what working people call the "real world," he decided he would probably have a better chance at a challenging future if he went back and gave college another go.

Metro specializes in providing opportunity to people like him, people who want a second chance at college. So, he signed up.

This time he did very well.

It was still hard, maybe harder, and he and his family had to make lots of sacrifices to get it done. But he said, with a lot of conviction, it was worth it!

He also said something during his presentation that I thought was wonderfully put and that I plan to quote many times in the future. He was talking about how the one big difference for him at college this time around had been the quality of the advice and mentoring he received at Metro.

What he said will stick in my mind for a good long time: "It is so much easier to believe in yourself if you know someone else believes in you!"

I would submit this as the most fundamental of all leadership principles. How great to learn it early in life! If David treats others the way he was treated, he can't help but be successful.

How are you going to get the best I have to offer? By making me realize that you believe in me, therefore causing me to believe in myself. This will draw from me my best work, my best thinking and my very best effort. I will not be inhibited, I will not be embarrassed, I will not be denied. And you will have had a lot to do with it. That is real leadership, being the catalyst for me to be the best I can be.

Another educator, Bob James, once explained this to me in a slightly different way: "Help everyone around you see themselves in light of a strength of which they may be unsure or unaware, hopefully related to the person they dream of becoming."

That's a tall order because it requires you to know something about who the person "dreams of becoming," and you must take the time to discover and emphasize "strengths" that may be obvious or hidden. If you believe that another of the keys to true leadership is that "You can't rise to the top unless you take someone with you," then this becomes the basic formula for getting it done.

If we want to be valuable, or even invaluable, to our organization, we must be the kind of manager who develops others. We should always be thinking of how to bring out the best in everyone around us. That will make us unusual and invaluable!

Back to Basics, Billy

Once in a while, it pays to park all new concepts, and remember the essence of what we do as we try to be leaders.

Not long ago I got an email letter from a high school kid who for some reason had to read one of my editorials as part of an assignment for his English class, He wrote a nice letter thanking me for my part in helping with his research on how business and management work. He ended by saying that it all seemed pretty complicated: leading other people and all. He said he wasn't sure he could remember all the stuff required to be a good leader and manager when, after college, he expected to go into business.

Well Billy, it's not that hard. As a matter of fact, it's easy to spell out; the hard part comes in putting it into practice. I'll do the easy part and leave the hard part to you.

The problem: How do you get people to do what you want them to do so that they want to do it?

The answer: Make your project important to your people. Here is where it gets a-little harder. The basic truth is that we (or almost anyone) will take up a cause, project or problem if we see it as being in our best interest to do so. The trick to being a good leader is to somehow get people to make your problem into their problem.

So, Billy, as I see it, this is the formula:

Get to know every member of your team, individually. This takes some work. You can't expect to get to know someone well enough to know how to interest them in your project, without really getting to know him or her as a person. Your aim is to find out what goals they have for themselves. If you're really good at this, they will probably find out as much about you as you find out about them.

Sincerely help your team members achieve their goals. This means through assignments, education, counsel, etc. you make them absolutely sure that you care about their goals as much as you do about your own. This must be honest. The simple secret is that good people will buy into your goal to the extent it helps them achieve theirs. This is how you get the best work that a person can produce.

Share the problem and information fully. When we understand the situation and our part in the solving of a problem, we can contribute the best help we are capable of. We will want our contribution measured because we will know what we are doing and what the objective is.

Seek and accept ideas. Generally, the least successful leader is the one who knows he has all the good ideas. Good leaders create an atmosphere where ideas flow easily and freely.

Share success and credit easily. All outstanding leaders have this in common: They enjoy the success of others in their group much more than grabbing the spotlight for themselves.

Build team. Work to increase the respect and willingness to share that each member of your group has for the others. Sell the idea that the team wins with the individual and the individual rises with the team.

Remember this: The people hardest to find in today's business world and thus the most valuable are those who have the ability to grow others rather than shine themselves.

o o o

The Biggest Management Sin of All

How to lose your job or at least deserve to lose it.

When I was a kid, I loved baseball. I practiced all the time. Across the street from our house was an open field with a small backstop with some heavy chicken wire carelessly nailed up to keep at least some of the balls in the field. The base paths had ruts in them, worsened by rain, but they were base paths and we used them.

I would play catch with anyone. My dad got me a first-baseman's mitt, and so it was first base for me. I played catch all the time. I even played catch with our house, knocking wooden shingles off in the process and having to help my dad replace them. I could catch, throw and bat with any kid in the neighborhood.

I finally got on a team. I did pretty well during practice and was actually chosen to be the starting first baseman.

The day of the first game came, and I was really nervous. Our pitcher walked the first batter. The next batter hit a ball too short, they got the guy at second, threw to me for the double play and I dropped the ball. The coach, from the third-base dugout, hollered in his booming voice for me and everyone watching to hear, "Wiesner, you jerk, do that again and you can go play for your sister's team!"

I played three more games for that guy. Each time I got worse yips, and each time he screamed at me more. I started out thinking I had a good chance of being a real player and ended knowing that I would never be.

I can't blame that coach totally. I was probably never destined for the bigs, but he didn't help me at all to be successful in Little League.

Ever since, I have had an aversion to people who "raise their voice" to intimidate or belittle others. I don't think anyone should waste their time working for a shouter.

How we think about ourselves is our reality. If a boss is trying to lower your self-opinion or self-worth, find another boss.

I had one boss who sat at a desk on a raised platform so he could look down on you. He was a lousy boss.

I had another boss who would gather his entire management team once a week and then insult everyone bitterly in front of us all. He would tell the chief engineer, for example, that if he were paid in food for engineering ideas, he would starve. Another lousy boss who ran a company where people didn't stay long.

I had a captain teaching me how to run a boat last summer, and all he would do is holler at me and make me feel like I would never learn. I fooled him. I got rid of him, and I learned from someone else.

I heard the other day that a friend of mine here in Denver is a shouter, a belittler, when no visitors are around. What a shame if it's true.

Worst of all is the damage we do to kids with this sort of thing. We change their lives by causing them to doubt their ability and their natural gifts.

What makes it even worse is that it is almost an irreversible event. Once you have made someone feel really negative about himself, how long would it take to reverse that feeling? Pretty tough to do.

My belief is that if we get caught shouting at people, demeaning them in any way, we should be fired. On the spot.

When a Manager Becomes a Scorekeeper

It might well be time to reevaluate one's ability to manage. Business decisions made based on the score will be much weaker than those based on the potential of the team and its members.

In the *Boston Globe*, explaining why he left the best job in industrial publishing, Terry McDermott, ex-president of the $800 million Cahners Publishing Co., said, "I started as a player, then became a player-coach, then a coach and then a scorekeeper. I didn't want to be a scorekeeper."

It happens that I knew Terry 25 years ago when he started as an advertising salesman in Chicago. It was clear from the beginning that he would be on a fast track. In the very short time (in career terms) of 15 years, he rose to the top of what was, at least then, the biggest and best trade publishing company in the country. His trademark was his strength, his hands-on approach, his touch with the people, his ability to understand based on his own personal experience and his genius for making his success from the combined success of everyone around him and throughout the organization.

What makes a guy like that quit at the top of his game with the best job in his industry? We only can speculate in this specific case, but there is a lot we can learn about leadership and management from what McDermott says.

While a "player," whether in sales, production or accounting, a person learns the importance and value of team and interdependence. It is almost impossible for an individual to succeed unless the entire group succeeds. The player who tries to prosper alone, or without regard to team, will one day wonder why he or she never got anywhere.

The player who advances to "player-coach" is one who realizes that understanding people, understanding what makes the rest of the team tick, is what counts. That player-coach understands that helping others succeed is what energizes the team to achieve results greater than the sum of what each could do separately.

The fully developed head coach can get the best work out of a group of people. The coach is interested in the development and well-being of every member of the team. As a result of the confidence and comfort this builds in the management team, each manager in turn builds the same feelings in each subteam.

Sometimes, the pressure to perform makes a coach become a scorekeeper. A scorekeeper is someone who judges everything and everyone by the numbers. The idea is that a person is as developed as he or she is going to get, and performance can be measured, quantified and graded. Improvement and growth are valid concepts but are left to the human relations department to implement.

Urgency from above causes the development of scorekeepers at all levels in an organization. A fully developed scorekeeper can cut the heart out of a motivated team. Scorekeepers are horrified by the prospect of a momentary sag in return on investment or internal rate of return that causes the constantly moving spotlight of good management to hesitate on them. They are often frozen into doe-like indecision by the headlights of a possible "career-crashing" decision, and they retreat into the personal safety of numbers in a way that cannot be traced, to the detriment of the company.

Well-run businesses need scorekeepers, but don't let them be in charge of people you expect to be motivated to work their very best for you and, in turn, get the best work from everyone in the company. If you feel yourself becoming a scorekeeper, stop to think just what it was that got you this far. And go back to it.

o o o

Forget Sales Technique!

Here's a better formula for successful selling

This might be too strong a statement, but the longer I am in selling, the more convinced I have become that attitude trumps technique.

Certain attitudes, that is.

During the first five years of my sales career I spent a lot of time learning sales technique, and I swore by it! I was well-trained, ambitious, hardworking and successful. I knew seven ways to get the prospect's attention and nine trial closes. I was a classroom expert in handling objections, having mastered techniques for flushing out the real objection, burying false objections, and I had memorized key responses to the 75 most common objections prospects had to our product. I knew the difference between the Presumptive close and the Puppy Dog close, and I knew the five great rules of selling.

I was ready!

Since those early days I have been to dozens of sales seminars, each encouraging me to learn "Six ways to do this" and "Ten ways to do that." I had a rule for how long to wait in the lobby for a customer, rules for writing follow-up letters and even a rule for how many times to take "no" for an answer before giving up. A real pro!

I knew lots of ways to handle objections. I used "feel/felt/found" every time I could ("Mr. Big, I know how you feel. So and so felt the same way until he finally used our product. He found that it worked perfectly"). I knew my product well, and objections were my friend. When one was raised, I would wade in and prove that we were right and the client had it wrong. And I sold a lot of product.

But over the years I kept running into people who were doing better than I was. What was worse, they didn't know all that stuff that I knew about the right way to sell. I wanted to know what they were doing that I wasn't.

What I found was that the people who were doing better were doing it with a better attitude rather than with irresistible technique. What made this attitude so powerful was that it was customer-centered rather than sales-centered. Dr. Benjamin Spock, who wrote the immensely popular *Baby and*

Child Care book many years ago, put it best when he said, "It is often better to put down the book and pick up the baby!"

Given a competitive product, what is stronger than superb sales technique is true and genuine concern for the customer and his/her problems. If I honestly believe that you are truly trying to help me solve my problems and not just trying to sell me your product, I will listen to what you have to say and give you an honest shot at the business I place.

The problem for most of us salespeople is that we sound like all we care about is our sale. We seem to always lead with ourselves and always talk about ourselves. "I'd like some of your time to tell you how you can save money using our product." Or, "I'd like to come by, give you my card and ask a few questions about your business."

Here are some things to try to develop an attitude that comes across better than technique:

Learn about your client. If you are calling on me and you don't know beans about me or my company, I'll know for sure that all you care about is your sale. Use the internet, your contacts and knowledge of the industry to find out more than any competitive salesperson could possibly know about your customer.

Bring more to the first (and every) meeting than your product. If all you do is talk about your product, you sound like all the other weak salespeople. I have problems. Come with an idea for me and we'll talk about your products later.

Be curious. Good salespeople don't have to make much of a presentation or worry how to handle objections if they ask lots of questions aimed at learning enough to solve customer problems.

Really get into your customer, and technique will take care of itself.

o o o

The Best Business Decision
I Ever Made

The fun of going into business for yourself

Now that I'm sort of retired, someone asked me the other day what I thought was the best business decision I ever made. Tough question.

Fortunately for me, the best decision I've ever made wasn't the result of some excruciatingly difficult moral dilemma or some painful lesson learned the hard way.

It came about rather innocently, kind of by accident or default.

It happened early in my business life and is a concept that has been responsible in no small part for whatever success this company has had.

Wiesner Publishing was started on a shoestring. I had been "consulting" for about three years after my last real job and I had decided to try to start my own business. So, I leased a one-room office in old Littleton, Colorado, and outlined an idea for a magazine, *Private Cable*.

I couldn't afford to hire anyone, so I did everything myself. It was in the days of the first Apple computers, and I bought one and learned how to do my own circulation list. At the same time, I solicited articles and tried to sell advertising.

It's not the easiest trick to sell advertising in a magazine that doesn't yet exist, but it's also something I've learned many times since.

At the same time, I went to the State of Colorado to register a name for my new venture. My first try was the name LAMP Inc.

I wasn't going to tell anyone what the name stood for (Laugh A Minute Publishing!), but it was chosen to remind me that I never wanted to get into the kind of pressure cooker that I had left a couple years earlier.

The state, however, told me Colorado already had a LAMP Inc., and therefore I had to settle for the much less meaningful and mundane Wiesner Publishing. So much for the easy part.

That done, I went back to doing everything myself.

It occurred to me that I knew a couple of guys who knew a lot about the business and that they might be interested in joining a new company. One was a great editor, the other a great salesman. Just what I needed! So, we all got together, and fortunately for me they got excited about our prospects. We went into business together; I was a 60 percent owner and they were each 20 percent owners. At the time none of our equity positions was worth a dime except that they included a blueprint to achieve a dream we all had.

And so there it was: the best business decision I had ever made.

I didn't recognize it as the best business decision I ever made until years later, of course. But I had found good people and given them the opportunity they wanted.

The three of us worked as hard as was possible, giving more than we thought we had, and together we accomplished more than any one of us could have done by ourselves. We had a lot of fun; we struggled with failures and roundly enjoyed every little success.

We were totally engaged.

What at the time seemed the only sensible thing to do turned out to be the way the three founders ran the company. We looked for the best people we could find, got to know them well enough to know what they wanted out of a job, and then tried to set up a way for them to achieve their goals working for us. Basically, their goals became our goals. Better yet, we discovered that when the company's goals and employees' goals intertwine, everyone wins.

Acknowledgements

This book would not have been put together if it hadn't been for the insistence of a lot of interested, capable people. I had retired from Wiesner Publishing, Inc. and sold the company to my son Dan Wiesner. Some years later, Dan and I were having lunch for no particular reason and he started to push the idea that we should make a book out of the editorials I had written over the years for *ColoradoBiz* magazine.

"Why?" I asked. "All of those stories have already been published in the magazine."

He said, "Yes, but every one of them makes more sense to the people that read them as time goes on. It's really good stuff. And when they're packaged together, they tend to reinforce each other making them even more valuable today. Let's do a book!"

After more conversation, we agreed to look into it further.

The first person I asked for an opinion was my wife, Janet. We had just celebrated our 60th wedding anniversary and she has always been my number one consultant in everything we have ever done. After she looked it over, she thought it was a great idea and said, "Let's do a book!"

We never would have had the quality product we ended up with if we hadn't had the really solid and detailed work of Eliza Cross, a good friend from the publishing business who has written a dozen books. We had expert design help from Laura Pilz, who knows all the secrets of making a book look great.

In the beginning, much of the initial work was done by interested and helpful family members.

Mike Wiesner helped a lot by listening to me talk about what we were doing. He was also a great source of title suggestions.

Sue Hessler did massive amounts of typing, organizing and reading. Computer solutions and time-saving ideas came from John Wiesner. These two contributed so much to our processes that they saved us many months of work.

Every time I called for more book title names, a rush of ideas came in from Tom Wiesner and Doug Wiesner. Everybody helped.

So we decided to do a book!